TO DANCE WITH THE UNIVERSE

The Ripening of Consciousness

Hope Raymond

Palo Alto, California

copyright 2012

to the

Millennial Generation

CONTENTS

1

Consciousness and Humanity

CONSCIOUSNESS OF LIFE TODAY

Most of us live our lives following a humdrum daily ritual: an alarm rudely wakening us; getting kids dressed and fed; shuttling dishes to the dishwasher or sink; packing lunches; gathering together the diaper bag, lunches, homework, and jackets; whisking kids off to the babysitter and school; and putting in a day's work. Then we reverse the scenario. We drop by the babysitter; pick up kids from afterschool programs; put in a load of laundry while cooking dinner; eat; bathe the kids; help with homework; do dishes; and if you're lucky, maybe catch a show on TV or the iPad, and check Facebook, before turning in for the night.

This same scenario, with cultural variations, takes place in homes across the world. But each person's story is a little different, giving us something to share with family and friends, as well as with the larger world. We hear these stories in personal conversations, through Facebook and Twitter, TV, iPads, and the Internet. Then, usually unconsciously, we try to make sense of our world by drawing these stories together into a single story about how the world works.

Living Ideas

While we are trading personal stories with each other, a larger, unseen and unheard story is taking place behind the scenes: the agenda of the universe being lived out through humanity as a whole. Just as the stories of our lives have certain themes that are frequently played out, so do particular themes rise to the forefront of the universe's concern, according to its needs at any particular time of human history. These themes I call *living ideas* because they are thoughts generated by the universe that drive humanity to incarnate them in our world.

An example of a living idea is reflected in human questions on the forefront of our society today. Does *mother* refer to the woman whose DNA matches that of a particular infant? If so, does that mean an adoptive mother—or stepmother—is not a mother? Does *father* refer to the hunter and breadwinner? Where does that leave a woman who may also be a breadwinner, or the *only* breadwinner in the family? Who is the mother in a gay family of two men and a child? Or two women and a child? What does *marriage* mean if gender no longer defines it? What defines a family when all members are male, or female?

At the heart of these questions is a living idea that is challenging outgrown patterns of relationship. We are concerned about these relationships because the universe is concerned. Humanity has been assigned the role of bringing more consciousness to the questions, making us thinkers for the universe.

Though the universe *drives* humanity toward concerns that need special attention, humans *choose* how to address these concerns in the actualized world. The universe is pragmatic and goal oriented; humanity is rational and moral. As consciousness for the universe, humanity needs to bring the functions of both the universe and humanity to any given situation, choosing a course that moves in the direction needed by the universe, like a driver guiding a team of energetic horses. Humanity and the universe are interdependent; the universe provides direction and energy, and humanity provides consciousness and choice making.

Ideas are at the very core of life itself. A Nobel Prize-winning biologist[i] said an "abstract kingdom" of ideas rises above the biosphere, similar to the biosphere above the world of nonliving matter. Ideas spawn in the human brain and have the power to spread infectiously through human culture. Cultural ideas that spread like a virus from person to person are called *memes*.[ii]

Experiments performed on highly sensitive gauges during public ceremonies for Princess Diana after her death, and immediately after attacks on the World Trade Center,[iii] showed that collective reaction to stirring public events have a common effect. That is, when an emotional event leads to the conception of an idea in the mind of someone experiencing the event, that same idea often then arises in the minds of others.

When an idea emerges from the abstract kingdom at the interface of the seen and unseen worlds, it becomes a living idea, indicating a new level of consciousness breaking through old consciousness.

When the time is right in the created world for the emergence of a living idea—large or small, at any level of consciousness—the universe senses the readiness. The living idea often builds on a thought that has been growing through time (e.g., war), though sometimes it is a virginal idea (e.g., the Internet). The thought may be at any level of reality and in any form or structure of reality, but it's all just energy at different levels of reality. When a thought that is ripe for furtherance emerges newly in the world, it becomes a living idea.

Because of the universe's connection with humanity in psyche, humanity becomes fascinated by living ideas and often spreads them, but sometimes does not. It depends on the amount of energy vested in an idea; that is, how much consolidated energy from various parts of humanity adds to its weight. This differs greatly from one living idea to another because of differing levels of consciousness. Though energy is carried at all levels, the universe responds more passionately to innovative ideas at a new level than to old ideas; novelty garners more energy from the universe than tried-and-true ideas.

If humanity's consciousness falls on a bell curve, as I think it does, then the middle group—the average person—carries energy from the largest number of people, but not necessarily the most energy around a living idea. Fewer persons are drawn toward change and to letting go of the past, as most people are reluctant to risk jumping into something brand new. This is why incumbents are often reelected.

Yet, in the past few years this maxim has been turned on its head, as we have seen average persons carrying the most energy around a living idea in the Arab Spring and Occupy movements. When humanity becomes more conscious of living ideas, it will be able to choose whether or not, and how, to actualize them in a particular form at a new level of consciousness.

This book focuses on the most energized living ideas at the newest levels of consciousness, ideas that have become unstoppable. By observing them, we glimpse what is of greatest concern to the universe relative to human choices and actions as a species. This provides a course for humanity's cooperation in fulfilling its role as consciousness for the universe.

SOULF

Thoughts move from the abstract kingdom of ideas into our everyday world by means of *soulf*, a contraction of soul and self. Soul and self came into being at the time of the Big Bang, when the first two dimensions of space and time originated. Soul is associated with space, and self with time.

Whenever the moment is right in our world of space and time, whenever a particular idea is needed to be thought out in our world, self and soul combine their energies as soulf to generate that thought in the mind of humanity. Some humans will react to the idea and choose how to live it out in the world. At that point of human choice making, the appropriate particle-wave collapses into itself as a particle, actualizing the human choice. Particle-wave, soul-self, and memes may converge in this moment of choice making. Or perhaps they are all one and the same. In any case, after a living idea is released into the world, it can spread like pollen in the springtime.

Soulf is "not the life of a being, it is movement . . . without a being that performs that movement."[iv] Soulf is not the dancer, but the dance. Occasionally individuals are aware that a thought—or the dance—that comes to them is not really theirs, but instead comes from another dimension. However, most of the time we assume it is our own thought. Either way, the living idea brought into the world is from soulf and is lived out through parts of humanity.

9

What is Consciousness?

When we speak of *consciousness*, we evoke a whole range of differing meanings. Some believe that consciousness is "as fundamental as space, time, and matter, perhaps even more so."[v] Others regard the universe as being "one unbounded ocean of consciousness in motion."[vi] A scientist said,

> "It was very important that a long time ago, we made the decision to separate spirit from science. And so we were able to learn how to do science. But now we've learned, and we can take on the richer task of learning to do science when consciousness is part of the experiment."[vii]

For the purposes of this book, the new consciousness means to dance with the universe's movement, which requires a fundamental shift in our thinking. We must move from ego-centered, either/or thinking to position ourselves within the threshold between ego and soulf, where life can be seen as an organic whole. At that point of merging with consciousness, we view life more truly from the perspective of soulf, and can summon the strengths of both soulf and ego in the service of new consciousness. New consciousness is the greatest gift humanity can offer to the universe, as it supports natural patterning and can help keep our planet from human destruction, a gift no other species can give.

DEVELOPING CONSCIOUSNESS

Formative Stages in Consciousness Development

The development of humanity's consciousness can be understood by looking at the stages of human development in individuals, a process that has been mimicked by humanity as a whole.

The infancy stage, in which a child sees herself as an extension of her mother, was mimicked by humanity in animism, in which humanity identified with its natural surroundings, Mother Nature.

When a child reaches five or six, she enters the magical stage of playing with imaginary friends, dressing up and pretending, and becoming mesmerized by fantasy tales of Cinderella, Jack and the Beanstalk, and Snow White.

Humanity, too, entered a magical stage when people started to differentiate from their surroundings. Instead of identifying with Mother Nature, they began to envision magical spirits in the natural world that could help or harm them. They tried to curry the favor of these spirits through their actions, hoping to affect their fate.

As children approach teenage years, their interest turns toward mythological tales, stories about gods and goddesses or other mythological-type characters. Many of the most popular video games and apps feature mythological characters and their heroic feats.

Over time, humanity as a whole also turned toward the mythological world. They believed the spirits had left their world and had become a colony of gods and goddesses in the heavens. Animism had morphed into mythology.

Later, monotheism challenged polytheism, but the effect was the same: the gods/goddesses—or God—seemed to be looking down on humanity, judging and controlling human activity. Unless people pleased them, the celestial beings might not protect them and respond to their needs. This belief prompted their offering of sacrifices and prayers, hoping to appease God and abate His wrath. Sometimes it worked; sometimes it didn't.

For centuries, these beliefs have remained in play for most people in the Western world and have formed the unquestioned worldview, the paradigm that shaped every thought and action. We knew the rules of the game, and it was up to us to abide by them. Though God was unpredictable and sometimes seemingly unfair, at least we knew someone was in charge and had a plan, and we were at the center of it. That was enough.

> "If it's personal, we call it an attitude—if it's cultural, we call it a paradigm—if it's universal, we call it a law." — *What the Bleep Do We Know?*[viii]

Like a horse balking at a stream of water, most of humanity keeps clinging to mythological/religious consciousness, refusing to proceed into adulthood with soulf. Life has moved on with the few who are willing to risk something new, while most of humanity stays behind in teenage consciousness.

New Consciousness

The new consciousness of adulthood contains everything that was there before: all the previous levels of consciousness. Everything that has ever been in any form of consciousness—and more—still resides within us.

The more refers to the merging of soulf with humanity. This occurred when truer understandings of the universe—especially Earth's no longer being seen as the center of the universe—were shaped during the Enlightenment. At that time, the mythological/religious world began to dissolve within us, but nothing was lost or left behind in the process. Everything humanity has ever experienced from mythology and religion still resides within humanity, including all the attributes of God. They are fully present, much as a sugar cube dissolved in a cup of coffee.

Dissolution of the mythological/religious world brought with it potential awareness of our oneness—our total oneness—with soulf, and all the authority, power and responsibility that go with it. Everything we need to live this reality resides within us.

Humanity's Adulthood

Today humanity teeters on the brink of adulthood. It has moved through the magical childhood years of religion; has weathered storms during the rebellious teenage years of science; and is now poised to plunge into the scary world of adulthood, where it must fend for itself. Humanity can no longer look to a heavenly Parent for rescue from the travails of life. The elephant brought into the room by science cannot go unnoticed much longer. Humanity is now on its own to make choices that can affect the whole future of the universe.

The death of religious/mythological consciousness, the death of God, is the birth of humanity's adulthood.

"The greatest problem we as a human race have is accepting our own questions. We run screaming from anybody who would suggest that we are all-powerful in ourselves." — Micael Ledwith[ix]

It is no wonder that many people still cling to the comfort of religion and refuse to face the findings of science. The power we hold is daunting to admit, and even more daunting to exert. Yet that is the task that faces us today. The sooner we accept the challenges it offers, the more fully we will be living out humanity's fundamental role as consciousness for the universe.

Humanity in its new psychological state contains all the understandings of both religion and science, which have converged with psychology at a higher level of consciousness. The stream of consciousness continues to evolve and wend its way through events, relationships, and processes in our world today. Humanity merely needs to relax and let go, enter that stream consciously, and move with it as it continues to evolve.

Consciousness in Humanity as a Whole

Perhaps the earliest signs of consciousness in humanity as a whole came in the form of religious rituals. Originally, ritual behavior was largely instinctual, but through time, collective consciousness developed, and much later, what we would call *individual consciousness*. Only in the past century or two has consciousness taken a further step, in which humanity has become conscious of its own consciousness. This was enabled by the rise of modern science, which corrected our perceived place in the universe, and furthered by images of our blue Planet Earth seen from outer space.

As scientists expanded exploration to the innermost regions of life at the subatomic level, they found an amazingly close relationship between thoughts in humans at their level of the universe and the behavior of particle-waves at the quantum level. This led scientists to see the crucial role of human choice making and consciousness in evolution, the primary process of life. If it seems difficult to believe in such a close mind-body connection, consider the fact that one sexual fantasy can trigger an erection.

This insight has required scientists to rethink their demeaning attitude toward the highly significant role consciousness has played in the field of psychology. Science and psychology have now moved closer together, and psychology's status has morphed from inferior stepchild to wise crone. However, this new role is not always openly accepted by the scientific community.

The stream of living consciousness has been working out is own development in human history by moving through religious thought, to scientific thought, and now to psychological thought. Finally—at least for humanity—consciousness has established its home within *homo sapiens*, furthering its own development there until humanity will have carried it as far as it is able. At that point, a new species most likely will develop to carry the stream of consciousness onward.

Abstractualization

Abstractualization (a combination of abstract and actual) is perhaps the newest and most pervasive means of consciousness development.

For years, psychologists have known about projection as a psychological phenomenon in which people see outside themselves qualities that exist within themselves. For instance, when we fall in love, we see attributes in our beloved that are undeveloped qualities within ourselves. Or, if we hate with a passion a politician whom we feel is responsible for everything that's going wrong in Washington, we are seeing within that person ugly parts of ourselves that we'd rather not face directly. In both instances our own reality has been projected outside ourselves.

The material creations of humanity—such as paintings, books, buildings, tools, and other sorts of cultural works, which are all actualized forms of ideas from within us—are almost a reverse form of projection. In the case of material creations, an abstraction (an idea, feeling, or attitude) within the psyche is projected, or created in material form, in the outside world. In projection, an abstraction within the psyche is projected onto an already-existing material form in the outside world. In both cases, the abstraction is externalized into a material form, shaping the living world we see and in which we live, which is somewhat different for each one of us.

Consciousness has now reached the point where we own many of the material actualizations we have created. They have become a digested part of us, so we no longer need to keep them in the material world.

This is where abstractualization enters the picture. Living ideas that were formerly actualized and housed in material form outside us are now being abstracted and given virtual form, often a digitized one. We can literally observe the disappearance of many actualized forms: music stores, books, telephone booths, magazines, maps, newspapers, filing cabinets, U.S. mail boxes, handwritten letters, CDs, and voting booths, to name a few. They are disappearing from our material world, but the living ideas they contain continue to exist in new, virtual forms. The living ideas of the actualized material forms have been abstracted and housed in nonmaterial forms, a process I call abstractualization.

Levels of Reality

Scientific experiments revealed a hierarchical universe that has many different levels and structures of reality. Levels comprise enveloping regions of depth, each new level surrounding the next deeper one.

When a process at one level gets new properties, it has to move to a new level. When it moves to that new level, it can be understood only at that level.

For example, a flock of birds is not the same as a few birds. The level of a flock has its own inner structure that is not present in a few birds hopping around in your back garden. They represent two different levels of reality. What determines the various levels of reality is not the composition but the structure.

Another example is the world wide web. The web has its own inner structure that is not present in the material creations from which its contents have been abstracted. They represent different levels of reality.

Levels of reality span the range from things to no-things: from subatomic particle-waves to the war in Afghanistan, from consciousness to concrete pavement.

Everything is part of the same reality, just at different levels of being.

Human actions are connected to the universe at the vibrational level. Everything of the same frequency responds to these actions, helping to shape our reality. In fact, all levels of vibration are affected to some extent by our choices of action, as "quantum [i.e., non-local] computations in our brains connect our consciousness to the 'funda-mental' universe."[x] Quantum uncertainty underlies the operating system of the human brain, opening the possibility for choice. Having free will, we can train ourselves to make smart choices.

In conjunction with human choice, a particular (particul-ar) particle-wave collapses and becomes a particle; that is, it becomes an actualized reality in our world of substance. Prior to that, as a particle-wave, it was merely one possibility among many, still in a world of nonexistence. Human choice decided which of all those possibilities to actualize, and that particle-wave responded accordingly.

Depending on our choice, cell connectors retain, or let go of, old patterns by hooking or unhooking other nerve cells. This process either retains old consciousness or generates a new form of consciousness. If we release old patterns, the new living idea unhooked by our choice jumps from one level to a higher one without experiencing anything in between. And all this is engineered at the quantum level of particle-waves!

"From the stance of new consciousness, our personal world is but one thread of a universal web . . . To engage with reality, we must see our connection to each other biologically, to our

world chemically, and to the universe atomically."
— Source unknown

Energy

Though energy—nothing but energy—is within all levels and structures of the universe, it manifests itself in a variety of forms, from physical energy to seemingly solid energy to thoughts.

A basic structure for many forms of energy is *opposition*. Two examples are the oppositely charged particles that balance one another by electromagnetism, and the opposite spirals of the double helix structure of the DNA molecule.

An even more dramatic example is the universe itself, which began and will end (if it ends) with opposites: "Billions of years ago the universe was too hot for life to exist. Countless eons hence, it will become so cold and empty that life, no matter how ingenious, will perish."[xi]

"The alternative to this big chill is a big crunch. If the mass of the universe is large enough, gravity will eventually reverse the expansion, and all matter and energy will be reunited."[xii]

Scientists today believe, in general, that the energy in behavior is what matters most. The fundamental reality of the universe is the behavior of energy in relationships, processes, and events, not bits of physical matter. As long as physical matter was seen as the foundation of the universe, science and religion could not be reconciled. "It was that extreme separation from the spirit world that enabled Western science to discover that mind and matter are the same thing."[xiii] Energy is at the heart of both science and religion. From that understanding, it was a mere hop, skip, and a jump for consciousness to assume its primary role today.

Humanity and the Cosmic Soup

Today the overall health and evolutionary well-being of the entire universe are at stake, depending on humanity's choice of retaining old consciousness or raising consciousness to a higher level. Only humanity can make that crucial choice because living ideas, powerful as they are, do not necessarily supersede human free will.

The choice of new consciousness is needed to calibrate the course of the unfolding universe. When that is figured out, humanity will be in a better position to combine its unique gifts with those of the universe to make wise decisions for today's world and its future.

Some may wonder why we should care so much about the needs of the universe when we have so many pressing problems of our own: economic woes, wars that never cease, polarization of politics, moral degradation—the list is endless. Yet these problems are in no way diminished in importance by refocusing ourselves on the health and evolution of the universe. The universe is a single organism, which includes you and me. We are all in the soup together. People here at home and those in the most remote areas of the world, friends and enemies alike; all the animals and birds and insects; even mountains and rivers; as well as the moon, the sun, the stars, the Milky Way, and galaxies thousands of light years away—we are *all* in the cosmic soup together. Whatever affects one part affects us all. As we know, the mere flutter of butterfly wings in Beijing can affect the weather pattern here at home. This being the case, how can we doubt the affect humanity's actions have on other parts of the universe?

Consistent with the patterning of the universe, when the environment is sick, so are we; disease and good health are both growing at the same time; physical and mental problems are inseparable; whatever affects the world around us affects us, and vice versa. Our human task is to work with the given situation as holistically and effectively as possible in order to foster planetary health. Our choiceful and wise actions can determine a thriving life community.

Primary Concerns of the Universe

In seeking to discover how humanity can best live in harmony with the universe, I have spent the past several years mulling over current events, relationships, and processes in our world, in search of living ideas from the universe. From the many ideas gleaned, I selected the few that exhibit the greatest intensity, those that rise up in the world today relentlessly and ubiquitously. These living ideas shape the form and text of this book.

At this moment of history, the two primary concerns of the universe relative to humanity are (1) assuring that human consciousness continues to evolve quickly enough to keep abreast of patterns of creation, including human cultural developments, that are rapidly becoming more complex and (2) preserving the universe as an organic whole that can continue to evolve and expand. For humanity, this translates into keeping Planet Earth in proper relationship to and in balance with the rest of the created world. The following chapters focus on these two primary concerns, with supporting data from current events, processes, and ideas prevalent in our world today.

21

A WORD OF PREPARATION

What follows is not just about linear movement, progression from one development to another, or events causing other events, though the desire to see the material that way may be great. The main concern is the non-linear movement of soulf within those developments and events.

But this presents a dilemma. One can write about timeless concepts, but how to encase these concepts within real-time events—except in poetry, dance, or another art form? Because of this conundrum, time frames are included in this book more frequently than I would have liked, but only for the purpose of clear communication.

In addition, names of quoted persons and sources are omitted from the text, for the most part, because these are of no more concern to the universe than time frames. Seen from the perspective of the universe, significant movements of humanity occur outside of time and are intertwined. It makes no difference who or what is instrumental in furthering living ideas and accomplishing the goals of the universe. It is humanity's task as a whole, as a species, to achieve what the universe needs. That's all that matters.

2

Development of Consciousness

The concern of the universe for speedy evolution of human consciousness manifests in two primary ways: through actions of the universe and through actions of humanity. Both are needed for the specific capabilities they have to offer.

ROLE OF THE UNIVERSE

Brain Development in Humanity

Human beings are uniquely designed to be intelligent animals. Creatures much smaller than humans could not develop the complexity necessary for intelligence; much larger ones would be limited by the time it takes information to travel across their brains. As in "Goldilocks and the Three Bears," we are just the right size.

Throughout history, evolution has favored human brain development. While the rate of overall human evolutionary change has been continually increasing, rising to more than a hundred times historical levels, the brain has been evolving at a faster rate than any other part of the human body. At the same time, the onset of puberty has been occurring earlier, and humans have had increasingly better health and longer lives, offering nature more time to evolve the human brain. All of this paves the way for higher consciousness, which is needed by the universe today.

As the human brain has evolved, it has kept growing in size and is an intricate example of complexity. It is like a map of the United States. At first, that map had just the bare markings of territories and a few states, but as the country grew, more intricate and complex markings could be added: state highways, local roads, and even little cul-de-sacs, all connected to one another. With its growing size, the brain is able to absorb increasing amounts of information at a fast enough rate to handle the greater complexities of today's world.

Another factor comes into play when considering our larger brains. Researchers examining variants of DNA have found that genetic evolution and brain size are directly related to population growth. The human brain would not have developed to its current size without a high rate of population growth. The human population is greater in size than is any other animal species, so the human brain— notably the frontal lobe—is larger than other animal brains.

As the human population grows in number, its genes evolve faster, and the fastest-evolving genes are those related to development of the human brain. According to a British anthropologist, Robin Dunbar, brains evolve and get bigger in order to handle the complexities of larger social groups. Considering globalization and the fact that the Earth's population exceeded seven billion people just twelve years after reaching six billion, and is on course to tripling in size by 2100, humanity needs a larger brain to cope with the increasingly complicated issues of larger social groups.

Humans socialize in the largest groups of all primates because our brains are large enough to handle the concurrent complexities. Dunbar says 150 is the upper limit to the number of individuals with whom we can have a genuinely social relationship. Creating a contagious movement usually requires the creation of many small movements first.

A number of people believe the rate of human population growth, which has recently been doubling approximately every fifty years, is at the core of many problems confronting us today. Among these problems are global warming, race relations, poverty, and crime. Yet during five years of collecting data for this book, not one news item about population growth emerged—until the announcement of our reaching the 7 seven billion mark!

Could it be that the universe is not pushing the issue of population size because genes in the human brain must evolve faster to meet growing complexities in today's world? (The universe is pragmatic and amoral, following the course of least resistance toward its goal, with no capacity for rational or moral thinking.) If so, perhaps the brains of some twenty-first century children have genetically enlarged too rapidly for adaptation and gone out of control. Could this be related to the growing number of children who have ADD and ADHD—and perhaps even to those with autism?

Human Speed

Although we have no control over the fast rate of human brain development, we are assisting with its furtherance. Today most young people are attracted to electronic games; in fact, some even become addicted to them. Speed is at the heart of many of these games, forcing the brain to work faster and faster.

One example is Guitar Hero, in which the goal is to play electronic guitar songs of various levels of difficulty as fast as you can. Studies have shown that laparoscopic surgeons who play video games, such as Guitar Hero, are 27 percent faster at advanced surgical procedures and make 37 percent fewer errors than do those who do not play.

In fact, faster growth of the human brain and consciousness is reflected in the increased speed of almost

27

every aspect of our living—from computer games to multitasking to packed schedules to texting 24/7 to jumping from hyperlink to hyperlink.

Even Google has had to be concerned about speed, given the increase in the number of Internet searches through its website to several billion a day. Through experimentation, Google found the number of searches dropped off when the company injected a 400-millisecond delay—just the blink of an eye—into its delivery of search results. That small delay represents several hundred million dollars a year in potential revenue.

Another reflection of their concern about speed is Google's simple home page, which has a large amount of white space because white space loads instantaneously.

All these speedy actions and experiences may be taking place—unconsciously, of course—as a means of helping the human brain tackle the complex, quickly changing tasks needed by the universe in today's world.

Role of Humanity: Artificial Intelligence

Humanity has directly addressed the need for more complex thinking through the development of artificial intelligence (AI).

For several decades, humanity has experimented with increasingly sophisticated innovations that are leading toward the day when the brain of a machine (or more specifically, its microprocessor chip, which serves as the brain of most electronic devices) outperforms the human brain. The point at which AI matches the intelligence of the human brain is known in AI circles as *singularity*.

Singularity

Singularity was first reached in 1997 when a computer called Deep Blue won a chess match against the world's chess champion, Garry Kasparov. At first, people thought it was a fluke, or rigged. But Deep Blue continued to win chess matches.

In 2011, a newer computer, Watson, accomplished the difficult feat of winning a Jeopardy tournament. This convinced many people that it is merely a question of time before singularity becomes everyday reality.

William Saletan of *Slate* magazine reflected on this movement toward singularity as a cosmic game:

"When the cosmic game between humans and computers is complete, here's how the sequence of moves will read. In the opening, we evolved through engagement with nature. In the middle game, we projected our intelligence onto computers and co-evolved through engagement with them. In the endgame, we merged computers with our minds and bodies, bringing that projected intelligence back into ourselves. The distinction between human and artificial intelligence will turn out to have been artificial."[xiv]

In 2007, hundreds of Silicon Valley technologists and scientists came together at a conference called The Singularity Summit: AI and the Future of Humanity. Together they imagined a future of self-programming computers and brain implants that would allow humans to think at speeds nearing today's microprocessors. Future technological developments in AI would explode traditional assumptions about the limitations of the human mind. In fact, a pioneer in AI[xv] said smarter-than-human intelligence is the future's only logical outcome. He even went so far as to set a date for it: 2029.

His thinking is not out of line. The number of transistors on a microprocessor chip doubles about every two years, while the entire evolution of modern humans from primates has resulted in only a threefold increase in brain capacity. Given the rapid advances in biotechnology and information technology, there is no scientific reason human thinking could not be pushed to speeds as much as a million times faster.

Taking in the ramifications of such a development, researchers at the AI conference warned that now is the time to develop ethical guidelines. Concerns ranged from amending the Geneva Convention with standards for the use of robots in the conduct of war to figuring out how to keep the future's super-intelligent machines from deciding to arm themselves to dealing with a self-improving, but amoral, AI that turns hostile.

Design of Microprocessor Chips

Many developments in microprocessor chips[xvi] have taken place in recent years. A major shift in design has made it possible for a billion transistors[xvii] to crowd onto a microprocessor the size of a fingernail.

Waiting in the wings may be an even greater breakthrough in chip design, one that uses electronic spin to carry information, instead of optical computing or nanochemistry. This emerging method has spawned a new field called Spintronics, which could herald a paradigm shift in microchip development.

In Spintronics, electrons travel without resistance and lose no energy, providing a way to carry more information than the most advanced silicon-based chips can handle. Electronic spin could surpass even nanotechnology,[xviii] which is currently used to build computers with almost unlimited memory.

Cognitive Computing

The federal government has shown considerable interest in these new possibilities and has funded studies of so-called cognitive computing. As part of the government's effort, IBM and Lawrence Berkeley National Laboratory joined together to perform a computer simulation that matches the scale and complexity of a cat's brain, surpassing earlier studies that simulated the much simpler brain structure of a creature the size of a mouse. IBM also joined with Stanford University to develop an algorithm for mapping the human brain at new levels of detail. These two projects may lead to a computer that mimics a human brain.

Currently computers are designed on a model that differentiates between processing and storing data. The human brain, however, can integrate and react to a constant stream of sensory information. A project manager[xix] at IBM who sees the need for a new kind of intelligence has been quoted as saying, "As our digital and physical worlds collide, there is a tsunami of information . . . There is a need for a new kind of intelligence that can sort through, prioritize and extract the most important information, much like how the brain deals with sight, sounds, tastes, touch and smell."[xx]

Connections of the Psyche

A significant development relative to cognition and choice making was chips that enable patients to control prosthetic arms using only their thoughts. By rerouting nerves from an amputated arm to the chest muscles, arms can move almost as fast and accurately as healthy arms when a patient thinks about moving them. The motions operate electrically, as contrasted with older types of prosthetic arms, which are biomechanical.

Paralytics are fitted with brain-reading gadgets that let them change TV stations, turn on lights, and write on a computer merely by thinking about doing those activities. In a game called Force Trainer, players move real objects by wearing a headset that reads their brainwaves. Researchers hope eventually to produce a chip-controlled brain device to help boost the memories of Alzheimer patients.

Similar technology is being used by the military to develop a thought helmet. The U.S. Army awarded $4 million to three universities to study how to harness brain waves to send nonverbal messages on the battlefield. The thought helmet, fitted with a microprocessor chip, would record electrical impulses from the soldier's brain for silent communication. As improbable as it sounds, *synthetic telepathy*, as the technology is called, is getting closer to battlefield reality.

In conjunction with research on thought-controlled devices, Intel is working with scientists at Carnegie Mellon University to decipher human brain patterns. "By analyzing the brain's electrical activity and blood flow when people ponder certain words and actions, scientists have identified patterns that computers can be programmed to read."[xxi] Researchers are now moving toward placing a nanosize microchip inside the human skull for faster, clearer reading of thoughts and to provide ready access to information on the Internet without any other device.

Connections from psyche to psyche may be the next frontier. An individual could access the consciousness of another individual directly, similar to the way we now communicate via cell phone and other digital gadgets with anyone anywhere in the world at any time.

Going a step further, if all the contents of individual human psyches were available from a cloud in cyberspace, consciousness would be dramatically advanced. Just as all the information of various cultures, which used to be held in outer containers, has now been put on the Internet, so could all the information stored within human beings be released from their containers and stored in a cloud, where there would be virtually unlimited storage capacity. Consciousness could even reach the point of total accord with the pace of evolution, enabling humanity to move on the forefront of soulf's wave instead of lagging behind. As consciousness for the universe, humanity as a whole would be fulfilling its role—in spades!

> "If we could access the global information network simply by using the power of our thoughts, it would open up incredible new opportunities for computing technology."
>
> — Dean Pomerleau, Intel researcher[xxii]

Possible Dangers of Artificial Intelligence

The possibilities for human and artificial brains are immense, and so are its dangers. Some ethicists have raised concerns about brain-wave readings being admitted into court trials as evidence of a person's truthfulness. This "raises all kinds of issues around privacy," said a university philosopher.[xxiii] While recognizing the usefulness of controlling machines with one's mind, she cautioned, "every piece of technology can be used for good or for evil."[xxiv]

AI could outperform the human brain, raising the possibility of its choosing to make its own decisions and follow an undesirable course of action. This would be especially hazardous in warfare. Becoming its own decision maker, AI could also expose people's brains to malicious hackers, who might cause a fatal heart rhythm by compromising an implanted cardiac defibrillator.

Scientists are well aware of these hazards and recommend parameters be set before things get out of hand.

THE SIGNIFICANCE FOR SOULF

Given the push from the universe in human brain development, and advancement from human scientists in brain research and AI, the ability of consciousness to meet the complexities of today's world looks hopeful.

The one big open question is: Will the global family open itself to sufficient consciousness to choose a course of action that supports our world and the universe as a single organism? Or is humanity too ego centered to think in such expansive terms? Our choice in this matter is crucial.

3

Connecting Humanity and Culture

As important as evolutionary changes in humanity are, the universe needs more. Its primary concern is with humanity *as a whole*, which requires that people be connected with each other, and with the world, at a much deeper level.

In addition, all people must have equal opportunity to expand consciousness; otherwise the masses will be left behind in consciousness development. Humanity's level of consciousness (which falls on a bell curve) is determined by the masses, not by an elite few. Therefore, expanding the consciousness of the masses (at the middle of the bell curve) is critical for the universe.

CONNECTING PEOPLE WITH INFORMATION

To this end, energy moved humanity toward abstracting information from its containers in many different parts of the material world, and making this information available to everyone. Another way of saying this is: ideas that had become actualized were abstracted from the containers in which they were housed and given a new home in cyberspace. In addition, humans were energized to develop new ways information could be accessed from everywhere in the world by everyone.

By making information available across the board, consciousness was raised, rather than settling for a lowest common denominator. Humanity as a whole could then make wiser choices. That will not happen through a few enlightened individuals; it needs participation by the masses.

The Internet

In unconscious pursuit of this lofty goal, humanity became energized to release contents from its containers and to digitize it.

iTunes was one of the first to buy in, offering single pieces of music as downloads. By overcoming the huge psychological hurdle of separating a single piece of music from its container, iTunes paved the way for ubiquitous electronic transmissions in a world wide web, the Internet. The Internet is now pushing the edges of the world, much the same way the universe is expanding its outer edges, and humans are expanding the edges of consciousness.

Electrified by the concept of an Internet, different culture entities reached out to contribute to its development. The British Library announced it was digitizing up to 40 million pages of newspapers, dating back three and a half centuries, and would make the results fully searchable and accessible online. Google embarked on a huge project of scanning all the estimated 50 to 100 million books in the world and stocking the Internet with digital versions for the public at large. Google also helped through its counterintuitive vision that companies can reach maximum success by charging not as much but as little as possible, so the number of people served can reach enormous proportions. The World Economic Forum even hosted a global dialog through YouTube, asking: "What key action do you think countries, companies, or individuals should take to make the world a better place in 2008?"[xxv] The question engendered one million hits and hundreds of video replies.

Average people around the world were contributing information to the communication freeway, necessitating its continual enlargement as contents outgrew the size of its pathway. In 2007, YouTube consumed as much bandwidth as the entire Internet consumed in 2000. People downloaded 100 million files daily, a 1,000 percent increase over the course of just one year. This mushrooming of information was pushing the Internet to its limits. The thousands of networks stitched together required continual innovations and upgrading to meet the phenomenal growth—or *exaflood*—in data to avoid traffic jam.

> "It took two centuries to fill the shelves of the Library of Congress with more than 57 million manuscripts, 29 million books and periodicals, 12 million photographs, and more. Now, the world generates an equivalent amount of digital information nearly 100 times each day." — Bruce Mehlman and Larry Irving[xxvi]

Broadband

Then came broadband. Its high speed dramatically expanded and extended the information highway, easing traffic flow and having the capacity to reach small villages in remote areas of the world. Virtually everyone could now have access to the vast pool of information on the Internet. The drawback was lack of funds. However, countries throughout the world have given broadband a high priority, so in time the dream of broadband being available to virtually everyone will become reality.

The importance of broadband for connectivity is comparable to the linkage in transportation in the twentieth century when a web of railroads, highways, roads, and bridges was built to connect people across the United

States. Those, of course, were tangible connections; broadband is intangible. This high-speed Internet connectivity has been called the most transformational technological advance since the printing press. It is certainly the most important industry in the world today, though nipping at its heels is Google Fiber, a high-speed fiber network that will have speeds of one gigabit, more than 100 times as fast as the average broadband connection.

Mobile Computing

When contents were abstracted from books, newspapers, magazines, phone books, CDs, etcetera, the market started bursting with innovative electronic devices to access the abstracted information. Among the most popular was the iPhone, which paved the way for a smorgasbord of choices from the smartphone industry. Smartphones became an immediate hit because people could access information and friends regardless of where they happened to be at the moment.

Within a few months, applications (apps) flooded the market, fleshing out countless possibilities. At the rate apps have developed since then, millions could be available before long, with billions of downloads. As of 2014, the number of downloads worldwide is expected to reach about 77 billion.

Among the many apps already available is location-based services (LBS), which pinpoints a user's location. This innovation could significantly change the way we live on this planet, integrating the virtual into our everyday lives. When it comes to virtual reality and reality, it is no longer either/or but both/and; the line between the two has become blurred. We live in a real world that is wrapped in virtual data.

For instance, an app called Where finds the nearest movie theater, restaurant, or events around you. Another app tells you the name of mountains you can see from where you are. SkyMap identifies stars and constellations you see overhead, and Sit and Squat locates the nearest public bathroom.

More parents are using smartphone apps to entertain and watch their children. They download a rattle to soothe a fussy baby, provide trivia questions for their young children while waiting for a dental appointment, play Who Wants to Be a Millionaire? with their older kids, and entertain them by flipping through pictures of the kids and their dog. They even leave a smartphone by their sleeping baby when they are out of range of their regular baby monitor.

People are becoming so wedded to smartphones and other mobile electronic devices, such as iPods, iPads, and tablets of various kinds, that they can hardly conceive of living without them. A college freshman captured the feeling of many people when he said of his smartphone, "I can't live without it. It's like water or food." Clearly a new era of electronic devices has arrived. We now stand squarely in the age of mobile computing.

CONNECTING PEOPLE WITH EACH OTHER

Connecting humans and information through the Internet was helpful to the universe, but more was needed. Humans themselves had to be connected worldwide in order to become consciously aware of their oneness. So humanity was nudged to expand existing worldwide connections to include human relationships.

Connecting Through Social Websites

Finding a path of least resistance, driving energy gave birth to MySpace, Facebook, and other social websites, immediately drawing people around the world into their domain. As of 2011, 86 percent of American children (and 83 percent of adults) used social websites. Though parents often worry about their plugged-in teens, studies by the Kaiser Family Foundation found those youngsters appeared to be well adjusted and healthy. Electronics seem to be the path by which children today develop emotional bonds and their own identities. Moreover, those who spend the most time on social media sites tend to be the healthiest psychologically. The digital world may simply be a new, multidimensional place to form identities separate from those of parents, which has always been the work of adolescence, according to the studies.

Some people believe that when teens check out their Facebook page, it is really social interaction. Teens of past generations would spend time in malls, cafes, and talking on landlines, while today's teens hang out on social websites.

For years it was a maxim that new communication technologies isolate people from each other. However, a Pew Internet and American Life Project study showed the opposite: people who used the web or cell phones had larger and more diverse networks of confidantes than did those who did not. Technology actually encourages more communication with more people. Also, Internet use is often associated with engagement in public places, such as parks and cafes, where exposure to more diverse groups of people and points of view is increased. Technology appears to be a social adhesive rather than something driving us apart.

MySpace, the first social website of notoriety, peaked in the fall of 2008, but was soon overtaken by Facebook, which quickly became the biggest social network in the world. An analyst at RBC Capital Markets noted an important difference between the two: "MySpace is where you go to express yourself, while Facebook has been a place where you go for two-directional conversation."[xxvii] Clearly, Facebook had the power needed to connect person to person, because two-directional conversation is relationship, at the very heart of creation.

The founder of Facebook said the idea behind it is that "people want to share and stay connected with their friends and the people around them."[xxviii] Facebook had attracted more than 950 million active users as of 2012, with 40 percent of people on the Internet using it regularly. Facebook users continue to grow at a rate of 5 percent per month, with the average user spending almost an hour there each day and having 130 friends. Remember, Robin Dunbar said that 150 is the upper limit to the number of individuals with whom we can have a genuine social relationship and serve as an incubator for contagious messages. Average Facebook users fall within this limit, so they can—and do—spread messages virally.

Twitter is another form of social network sharing, in 140 characters or less, of what is on people's minds—right now. It reverses the usual notion of a group by sending a tweet with a group assembling itself around that, rather than a person creating the group she wants. As of 2012, Twitter had about140 million active users, with more than 70 percent of Twitter's tweets coming from outside the United States.

An ambitious project preserving Twitter's entire archive of public tweets (an estimated 50 million a day in 2010, but more than 400 million a day in 2012) was undertaken at the Library of Congress, where Martha

Anderson explained: "We're trying to figure out the best way to leave evidence for future generations of scholarship."[xxix] Twitter is useful because it is informal, so people drop their guard and are spontaneous. This provides a deeply personal insight into the daily lives of ordinary people on an unprecedented scale. Its value includes not only information about the lives of average individuals but human expression on a massive scale.

> "If you think of Google as the Internet's memory—the process that can access every image, sound and bit of knowledge that our collective online existence has generated and stored—then Twitter is its stream of consciousness." — David Sarno[xxx]

New Ventures in Collaborating

Collaboration through new forms of communication is promising for the universe, especially in terms of connecting people globally.

In the past, online learning consisted of automation of face-to face learning. Today's social media, in contrast, involves high levels of collaborative effort over broad geographical areas. People begin to sense that everyone is part of even the remotest areas of the world. "We can be with people all over the world at any time," said a professor at the Graduate Theological Union, "and this is changing consciousness."[xxxi]

Facebook can play an important role, as it allows for a "communitarian approach to teaching," said another professor. "With Facebook, we can communicate with an international community of students and scholars." She views Facebook as "a digital version of shooting the breeze around the company water cooler. Sometimes those water cooler conversations lead to innovations and important insights . . . the same is true with Facebook."[xxxii]

Research-Gate connects scientists, free of charge, to do collaborative research and learn from one another. More than 500,000 of the five to ten million scientists and researchers worldwide are registered users. The service accelerates research by minimizing redundant experiments and providing for active collaboration. It produces faster, better, and cheaper results.

Google upgraded Google Docs to enable as many as 50 people to work simultaneously on analyzing a sales problem with a spreadsheet, drafting a contract, or working together on some other piece of writing—in real time. The upgrade includes a built-in instant messenger, which fosters an ongoing conversation about the project being worked on.

University of California at Berkeley and Stanford University created a free website, MathOverflow.net, which is transforming math research. By linking questions and answers from the smartest minds around the most difficult math problems, "each small solution builds toward a larger understanding, accelerating research."[xxxiii] Having this repository of global knowledge demonstrates that mass collaboration can dramatically expand and speed up problem-solving abilities.

THE SIGNIFICANCE FOR SOULF

Contributions to the Internet from many sources have been a giant step in leveling humanity on a higher plane, and in making wise choices more possible for everyone. People in all countries and from all walks of life can connect with others across the globe and dip into the pool of wisdom from every culture throughout the ages. The long journey toward raising consciousness in humanity as a whole has begun.

CHAPTER

4

Dissolving Boundaries to Cohere Humanity

With expansion and openness of communication, centuries of encrusted boundaries began to dissolve and categories became blurred. Cosmic energy was drawing human beings closer to each other and to the natural world.

Throughout society, from journalism to social relationships, from animals to electronic devices, boundaries continue to crumble, making it necessary to rethink categories and meanings of words.

RELATIONSHIPS

Personal and Social Boundaries

Breaking of boundaries in personal and social relationships is occurring at an almost breathtaking rate.

Formality started going out of fashion several decades ago. Informality eased its way as Fridays became dress-down days, receptionists greeted visitors by their first name, and women wore pants to work. These trends have become so commonplace they no longer draw attention, but other areas are still in the process of deep change.

Gays and Lesbians

The daughter[xxxiv] of a former Secretary of Defense is a prime example of undergoing change. As a lesbian, she used a sperm donor; was pregnant out of wedlock; has a lesbian partner; and lives in Virginia, where same-sex marriage and civil unions are banned. Yet none of this rocked the boat in mainstream media. What had been a taboo was merely another day's news item.

Recently, acceptance of gays and lesbians has gained much traction. The armed forces broke down the barrier to those who are openly gay, several states legislated acceptance of gay marriages, and the majority of Americans say gay marriages should be legal. Gay story lines have become more prominent in movies, and bisexual, lesbian, and transgender characters are almost commonplace on television. California has gone so far as to legislate that history textbooks include discussion of the contributions of gays, bisexuals, and transgender people to the state and nation's history.

Sex

Explicit sex is no longer censored from the morning news, always spoken of euphemistically, or relegated to X-rated films. Media spokespersons unabashedly speak of oral sex, orgasm, condoms, and you-name-it. Sex in the City and Tell Me That You Love Me, which has been dubbed "the most sexually explicit show to ever air on mainstream TV,"[xxxv] leave the bedroom door open without a blush. The National Health Service of Sheffield, England, even sent a leaflet to schools likening the health benefits of eating fruits and vegetables, and exercising, to the benefits of masturbating twice a week. Their slogan was: "(A)n orgasm a day keeps the doctor away."[xxxvi]

Marriage

Living with a partner outside of marriage has become ho-hum, and unwed mothers hardly raise an eyebrow. In the United States, cohabitation continues to increase, while married households are now in the minority. As a senior fellow at the Brookings Institute said, "The culture is shifting, and marriage has almost become a luxury item, one that only the well-educated and well paid are interested in."xxxvii In some European countries with declining birthrates, this is especially true. People are more concerned with a newborn's health than with the marriage status of the parents.

As for fidelity in marriage, Americans act shocked and outraged when they hear about the adulterous affairs of a senator or other public figure, not to mention of a friend or spouse. However, they often overlook the fact that within the last decade, incidents of adultery have risen to 50 to 70 percent in America. Clearly something is amiss in a country where more than half the citizens engage in activities that are condemned by society. Either society needs to temper its rigid expectations or rethink the whole institution of marriage, and relationships in general.

With soulf's potent energy drawing people closer together by breaking down boundaries between them, marriage relationships are, of course, going to be affected, along with relationships in every other area of society.

Birth, Children, and Youth

Birth options have opened up, breaking boundaries that never before disclosed hidden possibilities. Ready-made embryos are available, and giving birth at an advanced age is possible, not to mention the proliferation of fertility clinics to guide people in choosing from an array of possibilities for becoming pregnant and giving birth.

Children and teenagers have lost all sense of privacy from their parents, as the modesty shield that used to provide some distance between them has been shattered. Today parents can check on their offspring around the clock via webcam, surveillance cameras, cell phones, Facebook, and GPS. Boundary breaking may be drawing

51

them closer together, but the long-term effect remains in question.

Changes in marriage, birth, and parenting options have surpassed the words we have to describe family relationships. Unconscious boundaries that have always encased clear meanings for *father* and *mother* have eroded, bringing into question not only what these words mean, but also other words that convey assumptions about the meaning of these terms.

Family Law

Some of these words occur in family law. Legal terminology has been deeply affected by changes in the way we see and experience relationships.

A dozen states have replaced *divorce* with *dissolution* because one person is no longer seen as innocent and the other as at fault. That boundary has been broken. *Alimony*, which used to refer to a man's support of his wife after divorce, has been replaced by *maintenance* and *support*, which are gender neutral. *Parenting time* is now sometimes used instead of *custody* and *visitation* to suggest equal importance of both parents.

U.S. family law, a mechanism for setting clear boundaries, has shifted to a higher level of consciousness.

Pets and Humans

The boundary between humanity and the natural world also is being dissolved. The relationship of humans and animals has become a path of least resistance in drawing humanity closer to other species and to the universe.

Animals frequently appear as human interest stories in the media, and more American households have pets than have children. Sometimes animals are mentioned first in headlines: "Pets, family escape bedroom blaze."

Pets may trump the family entirely by moving to center stage in both the headline and early coverage, leaving the family as almost an afterthought. In "Firefighters Rescue Dog from Fire that Ruins House," the news item read: "Fearing that people might still be inside the house . . . the first crew went in with water hoses and found a 'very affectionate' but frightened dog in a bedroom. It appeared to be a terrier . . . Four people had escaped from the house before or during the fire."[xxxviii]

Dogs have been upgraded from man's best friend to member of the family, as two-thirds of pet owners consider their pets family members. In keeping with their new status, legislation in some parts of the country now refers to those who have pets as *guardians* rather than *owners*. Both dogs and cats are welcome in most hotels, and PetSmart runs PetsHotels nationwide. The pet industry has become big business, expanded from $45 billion in 2006 to more than $56 billion in 2012, despite tough economic conditions.

Most dogs and cats now have human names, such as Max (which rates #1), leaving the Fidos, Snoopys, and Lassies to their ancestors. Many dogs and cats also have Facebook accounts and followers in Twitter.

The lifestyle of pets is starting to parallel the lifestyle of humans, a clear sign that pets have become a channel to draw humanity closer to the natural world.

OTHER AREAS OF BOUNDARY BREAKING

Personal Data

Dissolving boundaries extends to finances and other personal data that have traditionally been considered taboo for revelation, but are now being exposed to public view.

Pilot projects are exploring ways to support the general welfare by encouraging people to release personal data on the Internet. Projects include increasing charitable giving through releasing information about income and one's own charitable giving; reducing national gas usage by posting one's gas bill online; and sharing medical and educational data.

The cosmic energy behind openness and transparency is most widely visible through WikiLeaks, an amorphous network in more than a dozen countries that reveals classified documents. Their website says, "Publishing improves transparency, and this transparency creates a better society for all people."[xxxix]

Zoning

Urban and suburban areas undergoing redevelopment are now often freed from fixed zoning as exclusively business or residential and are allowed to become mixed-use developments. Condos, duplexes, coffee shops, townhouses, markets, and offices frequently cohabit redevelopment space.

Journalism

With the growing popularity of the Internet, journalists discovered that discrete news articles could no longer be framed; they needed to morph into an ongoing series of news dispatches on the web. Media acted on this finding, bringing journalism closer in alignment with the mode of the universe, which energizes happenings without boundaries.

Electronics

Electronics may exhibit the most obvious, though often unconscious, area of boundary breaking. An example is Google's interactive system that dissolves the wall between television and the Internet. Users can search TV the way they search the web, seeking out a specific piece of content, whether it is scheduled for a TV broadcast or a website video.

Virtually every electronic gadget today incorporates at least two or three functions. Smartphones have multiple functions, so many that the phone part has become almost irrelevant. People use smartphones to tweet friends, check stock market fluctuations, read a book, and find a restaurant, but much less often just for calling someone.

THE SIGNIFICANCE FOR SOULF

In many areas of life, the universe is prodding us to dissolve boundaries. Sometimes the prodding is subtle, other times more overt. Soulf uses whatever ways will work. The goal is to break down boundaries so humanity's consciousness is raised. Then humanity will recognize the entire universe—including all people—as a single organism and will act accordingly in decision making.

CHAPTER

5

Globalizing To Cohere Humanity

In addition to dissolving boundaries, energy began coalescing groups of people at every level and in every constituency of society—internationally, nationally, and publicly as well as socially and personally. The time was right for globalization, as the human brain and population size were becoming large enough to handle the complexities of living globally.

SIGNS OF GLOBALIZATION

An early wake-up call to globalization was a study showing that, during the spring, ozone from Asia wafts into Western United States, impeding attempts to clean up the air in states west of the Rocky Mountains. At the same time, emissions from the United States drift across the Atlantic and reach Europe. The ozone layer is a global problem.

Overt signs of globalizing—a slew of them—have become evident since then: Japanese car sales in California surpassing domestic models for the first time, gobbling up nearly 45 percent of the market; E-Trade Financial becoming the first U.S. discount brokerage to make it possible for American customers to trade foreign-listed stocks online; wealthy Chinese signing up for home-buying tours to the U.S., hoping to snag a good deal following the recession; McDonald's reaching out to the Asian population in Southern California by renovating its Hacienda Heights restaurant, with the consultation of experts in feng shui; and the Securities and Exchange Commission eliminating a requirement that foreign companies use U.S. accounting standards with their U.S.-

traded shares, and allowing them to choose between international and U.S. accounting standards.

Sharing Cultural Developments

Countries across the globe are reaching out to one other by offering aid and sharing cultural developments.

Telemedicine (which transfers medical information through interactive, audiovisual media for consulting, conducting examinations, and directing medical procedures) is becoming more widely available in cities and remote areas all over the globe. A South African company offers banking services via cell phone for the world's 5.5 billion unbanked poor people. Two graduate students in engineering developed NanoLab, a handheld laboratory to diagnose illness in remote places throughout the world. NanoLab is simple, easy to use, and can be taken anywhere.

One of the most ambitious projects in reaching out is One Laptop Per Child (OLPC). This project places low-cost, portable PCs in the hands of school children, hoping eventually to reach all developing countries. As of 2011, more than two million of its $200 laptops have been distributed to 42 countries worldwide. A study made by Inter-American Development Bank showed that greatly increased access to computers accelerated students' abstract reasoning and speed in processing information by about six months. Dutch researchers found similar improvements in a study made in Ethiopian schools. An official from Peru's Education Ministry called the abstract reasoning findings "spectacular." Abstract thought is essential for humans in developing a deeper, closer relationship with abstractions such as soulf and in working within our abstractualized world wide web.

OUTSOURCING

When the top tax rate in the U.S. was lowered in the 1980s, some people were able to accumulate a vast fortune in one fast deal. Executives got rich quick and left their companies. Long-term business plans went out the window, employees were cut, and companies took advantage of customers. In losing their interdependence with the community, businesses found they could become more profitable by outsourcing or selling off manufacturing.

People usually connect outsourcing with globalization, but they sometimes fail to see beyond its pluses (or minuses, depending on one's viewpoint) for the United States. Formerly, manufacturing was done in one location. Now it is often split between two places: one in the homeland for research and development, and another somewhere overseas to keep it going. For example, in Silicon Valley, a few, highly paid people do the innovating, and the work to keep it going is often sent overseas, a process that is similar to the separation of content from container. In both cases, global connections are made, helping to cohere humanity and the world. Another example:

"A colleague of mine recently needed a new bicycle light. He flipped on his computer, searched for a few minutes and found a good one for the right price. Using his PayPal account, he paid for the light and shipping costs, shut off his computer and went back to his day. It wasn't until later that he realized he had logged on in Berkeley, bought the light from an online company in Hong Kong, which had the light

61

assembled in inland China with parts made in the United States, and he had paid for it all thanks to a company headquartered in San Jose.

We suddenly live in a truly global world."[xl]

Outsourcing works in a variety of ways. During the recent recession, small U.S. newspapers felt the pinch of advertising dollars but needed to hire journalists, so some of them outsourced reporting.

One publisher ran the following ad in the Indian edition of Craigslist: "We seek a newspaper journalist based in India to report on the city government and political scene of Pasadena, California, U.S.A." He hired two reporters in India for about $21,000 and pointed out that weekly Pasadena City Council meetings could be watched over the Internet. "Whether you're at a desk in Pasadena or a desk in Mumbai, you're still just a phone call or e-mail away from the interview."[xli]

India's outsourcing giant, Infosys, developed a new model for global businesses. It hired young Americans, flew them to India for an intensive, six-month training program, and redeployed them to the United States. An Infosys vice president called it a "rewrite of the Industrial Revolution for the digital economy."[xlii] This model has been embraced by much of the tech world, and U.S. companies, such as IBM, Accenture, and Oracle, all go to India, where they hire engineers as fast as they can.

Outsourcing and the U.S. Debt Crisis

While India and China were busy growing their economies, the United States started importing more computers, high-tech components, and consumer electronics than they exported, jacking up the U.S. trade deficit in their industry to $102 billion. Some of these imports were from American companies that were designing chips in the United States, manufacturing them in their overseas plants, and then importing them. This process was a huge drag on the U.S. trade deficit, though it helped draw East and West closer together. A columnist spelled out his vision of the vicious cycle that led to the massive U.S. debt:

"We have created a system for growth that depended on our building more and more stores to sell more and more stuff made in more and more factories in China, powered by more and more coal that would cause more and more climate change but earn China more and more dollars to buy more and more U.S. T-bills so America would have more and more money to build more and more stores to sell more and more . . .

What if the crisis of 2008 represents something much more fundamental than a deep recession? What if it's telling us that the whole growth model . . . is unsustainable?"[xliii]

COLLABORATION

Collaboration has become increasingly team based and international with maturation of the Internet. People with a common interest, such as science and technology, have entered into collaborative research across the world in ways not possible before the end of the Cold War. Researchers now have shared access to the Internet and applications to connect them globally in real time. With these advantages, each scientist can build on the findings of others, speeding up research, with less duplication of experiments.

New possibilities include public to private ventures among both groups and individuals, providing a powerful tool for cohering humanity.

Collaboration of Groups

Cisco and Intel, among other companies, rearranged their office space to encourage collaboration, saving space and money at the same time. Until the latter half of the twentieth century, offices were discreet units with doors, providing absolute privacy. The norm gradually shifted to a large common space, broken up with individual cubicles. Now that form has morphed into open areas with armchairs, extra conference rooms, and tables workers can use for laptops. Employers find more work gets done in this space arrangement, and workers interact better as a team. Both are requirements to meet the challenges of an increasingly complex world.

An American biotech firm[xliv] linked up with a large Brazilian ethanol maker to develop clean fuel from Brazil's plentiful sugarcane. Using synthetic biology technology, they are creating renewable diesel for cars, trucks, jets and generators.

Universities, too, are experimenting with new ways of collaborating. As noted earlier, Stanford University joined with IBM to develop an algorithm for mapping the human brain in much greater detail than was done in the past.

Stanford also operates an innovative Bio-X program, which promotes collaborations between wide-ranging fields of scientists. The leader of the program said, "This is where the future of biomedical research is going—working at the interface of quantitative science, physics, engineering and biology."[xlv] Her prescience is evident in both the pure and applied research now taking place.

In support of collaborative ventures at Stanford, the university emptied books from both the physics and engineering libraries and replaced them with a smaller but more efficient bookless library. Because it is largely an electronic library, it can accommodate the "vast, expanding and interrelated literature of physics, computer science and engineering."[xlvi]

Public-Private Collaboration

Some scientists have broken the barrier between public and private spheres, and are engaged in ventures of collaboration between the two.

Google and NASA collaborated to monitor CO_2 pollution and forest destruction, two contributors to global warming. Their web program, EarthEngine, is essentially a massive storehouse of data from satellites and cyberspace that forested countries can access for free.

Google also partnered with the state of California on a project, Cal-Adapt, to show Californians how their environment is being affected by extremes in natural processes. This feature of GoogleEarth presents data regarding California's more frequent, intense wildfires; global warming; rising sea levels; and other extremes in nature.

Cities and counties have discovered the value of public-private collaboration. One widely used form is outsourcing city services to private contractors, in particular for paving roads, trimming trees, and collecting garbage. Some cities, including New York, have hired private conservancies and nonprofit groups or foundations to operate their parks.

Collaboration in public-private ventures now stretches across the continents. Cisco Systems collaborated with South Korea in building New Songdo City, designed for a million people. The city includes a hundred-acre park modeled after Central Park in Manhattan and is fully equipped with sophisticated technology.

Collaboration of Individuals

Individuals, too, are collaborating in various ways. Vanishing Point is an artificial reality game designed as a form of advertisement. Teams of strangers collaborated on the Internet to solve giant puzzles, with clues in widely scattered locations. Messages were hidden in a "Bill Gates speech, a light show that used the fountains outside the Bellagio Hotel in Las Vegas as a canvas for clues, skywritten messages above four cities, coded images projected onto the walls of various monuments and a fireworks extravaganza with a secret message in the skies above Seattle."[xlvii] In order to solve the puzzles, strangers in different parts of the United States needed to collaborate in providing answers to clues. The game drew 70,000 participants to the puzzles and more than twenty million page views at the Vanishing Point website.

Second Life is a website where a person (visually represented by one's choice of an avatar) enters a virtual world to explore, shop, go to restaurants, play games, see movies; that is, do the same things one would do in real life. Its members design the site's global community, working together to build a new online space for "creativity and collaboration." Second Lifers from all over the world use their inner authority to try out new choices; collaborate with others; and experiment in any way they wish, without fear of backlash. This opportunity to make mistakes without punishment and to collaborate with others can build confidence, broaden experience, and enable people to discover who they are as unique individuals. All are values energized by the universe.

Experiencing success and developing new interests in Second Life often transfer to real life. For example, people who have never been especially interested in the environment frequently become involved with environmental concerns in Second Life. Many report their experience there has led them to collaborate with others who are involved with environmental problems in real life.

THE SIGNIFICANCE FOR SOULF

We are bringing the world into ourselves—or more accurately, finding the world within us—where we can envision its unfolding. Increasing numbers of people are moved to share their vision with national and international communities. Globalizing is one of the most pervasive movements of soulf in the world today, with the goal of cohering humanity worldwide.

6

Fulfilling Individuals to Cohere Humanity

A third facet of coherence worldwide is enabling persons to fulfill their lives as individuals. Holding humanity together must include the common person—not just the powerful, highly educated, and famous—because consciousness of the masses determines the consciousness level of humanity. To move the consciousness of humanity to the next level, most people must claim power and authority from within themselves in order to mitigate the outer authority and power now held by the privileged few.

Arnold Schwarzenegger made a timely tribute to the common person when he arrived at the swearing in ceremony for his second term as governor of California, making his entrance to the soaring notes of Aaron Copland's Fanfare for the Common Man. This heralded the emergence of the average person, a movement that had been gaining momentum in the early years of the twenty-first century.

NEW STATUS OF "YOU"

Time magazine recognized the significance of what was happening by naming "YOU" as Person of the Year 2006, emphasizing the pronouncement with a mirror on its front cover. No mistaking that the editors meant YOU, whoever you are, the individual, average person, and that YOU now have VIP status. Synchronously, the issue was dated December 25th, symbolizing new birth or a Christmas gift to the common person, the Millennial Generation or the world at large.

The average human being is emerging from the teenage years of humanity and moving into young adulthood. For the first and only time, some individuals—

71

the Millennials—and humanity as a whole are entering adulthood simultaneously. *Time*'s Lev Grossman believes "an explosion of productivity and innovation" is taking place, as "millions of minds that would otherwise have drowned in obscurity" are now participants in the global intellectual economy. The twenty-first century could be called "the century of emergence of the individual."[xlviii]

This new birthing sprouted in many forms and places, encouraged by various segments of society.

DISCOVERING POWER AND AUTHORITY

Individuals are popping up everywhere, exercising newfound power and authority. Parents see individual needs in their children and summon inner authority to develop charter schools. Summer camps are catering to individual interests, shifting from generalist to specialized, and featuring tennis, art, computers, or the like—but only one of the above. Children are left to choose the area of their own particular interest.

Gift cards sprung up at Safeway, Walgreen, and Target to match one's personal taste. When a birthday, Christmas, or graduation comes along, no one knows better than the recipient what the perfect gift would be. Gift giving today puts a different slant on "It's the thought that counts."

MEDIA

Average people are affecting Internet content through their contributions to Wikipedia, the free Internet encyclopedia anyone can edit. Though questions arise regarding the qualifications of contributors, anonymity is considered responsible for Wikipedia's astonishing growth. It rivets the reader's attention on the substance of what people have written rather than on credentials.

No professional chef wrote any of the top ten bestselling cookbooks of 2006, and *Taste of Home*, the most popular food magazine in the United States, had more subscribers than *Gourmet*, *Food & Wine*, and *Bon Appetite* combined. When cooking, people shun the experts. They want to decide for themselves or learn from others like them. People turn aside chefs, such as Mario Batali, in favor of home-cooking Paula Deen and Rachael Ray, saying they want recipes from real home cooks for home-style, country, and everyday meals.

Carrying this trend even further, newspapers and other media now invite "You" to review the restaurant you go to. The *San Jose Mercury News* issued an invitation to the average reader: "We want you to have your say about some of the restaurants we review . . . Contribute your thoughts . . . We will print a selection of reader comments with [Aleta] Watson's review."

POLITICS

Web interaction between presidential candidates and average Americans started early in the campaigns for the 2008 election. Hillary Clinton had an ongoing relationship with Yahoo that included contributing to a blog on Yahoo Health. In blogging, she solicited ideas about ways to help prevent and eradicate breast cancer. It drew

4,890 responses from ordinary people. A spokesperson at George Washington University said, "So many people are used to politicians telling them what they think. In this case, it's the politician asking voters what they think and actually listening to the answers."[xlix] She said Clinton was showing that the Internet is the new town hall.

The Internet is, indeed, the new town hall. In 2008, Clinton, among other presidential candidates, met the average person face to face—well, not exactly, but avatar-to-avatar—on the website Second Life, where many ordinary folks were spending time.

Her town meetings there focused on an outdoor stage with a large, spotlighted picture of her as backdrop. Behind the stage, a police Humvee watched over a helipad and a long line of stretch limos, while avatars awaited her arrival. Kiosks sported Hillary golf shirts, and information on how to join her campaign dotted the surrounding area.

ENTERTAINMENT

American Idol

Text votes from the average person at home decide the winner of the immensely popular reality TV show, *American Idol*. "It says to the whole entertainment industry, 'You are not in control. We are,'" commented a cultural historian.[l]

Web Stars

Social networking sites have become the new conduits for celebrities. While more traditional sources are busily scanning the Internet for possible new stars, kids are creating their own web stars though text messaging and sound files. Teens are "tired of being force-fed the latest studio creation" and are waiting for an artist of their own choosing. When they find one, they spread the word within minutes throughout social websites. With YouTube and Facebook, no major label is needed to become famous.

Amateur Videos

The election of 2008 became known as the YouTube election because video clips from average Americans supplied most of the questions for the presidential debates. Nearly 5,000 video clips were submitted for the Republican debate, from which CNN chose about two dozen. The public at large viewed and rated potential questions before the debate, though CNN made the final decision about which clips to use.

A similar public invitation was issued to submit ideas for beer commercials for the Super Bowl, and the winners were exposed to tens of millions of viewers.

Amateur video making has been encouraged by the annual YouTube Video Awards, which recognize the best user-created videos. Who decides the winners? YouTube viewers, of course.

PERSONAL FULFILLMENT THROUGH SOCIAL WEBSITES

A growing number of websites provide space for self-expression, raising the status of individuals. Personal opinions, thoughts, photos and whatever else one chooses, can be put on the Internet for the entire world to see. Social websites such as Facebook, Twitter, YouTube and blogs provide a path of least resistance for soulf to energize the inner life and personal expression of the average person.

Facebook shows one's picture, biographical information, likes and dislikes, plus anything else one chooses to share with friends. Twitter acts as a stream of consciousness, recording whatever is on one's mind—right now—and puts it out to whoever is interested. YouTube is a way of sharing short videos with the general public through the Internet. A blog is a journal, a column, or thoughts shared with others on the Internet. All these opportunities for self-expression help individuals connect with inner authority and power, fostering self-esteem and opening the door to personal fulfillment.

INDIVIDUALS AND INSTITUTIONS

For some time, individuals have been showing less loyalty to institutions, in favor of making choices to fulfill their own lives. Lifetime marriage to one's job fell by the wayside when individuals started moving to a different company when it benefited them personally. This choice making reveals a new connection with inner authority and power.

A different generation of politicians with less loyalty to their own political party has endangered incumbents, who need strong party backing. A devastating example for the Republican Party was its Tea Party members. Despite their relatively small number, they managed to upset the applecart.

Shareholders in stock companies are showing less loyalty to the recommendations of boards of directors. In stepping up proxy resolutions, they netted a 59 percent success rate. A Bear Stearns analyst commented on the success of a shareholder resolution that triggered a 9 percent jump in Applebee shares: "Our immediate reaction is one of surprise that the long-term course of this company could be altered by pressure from a relatively small activist shareholder."[li] But it happened.

SOCIAL ENTREPRENEURS

Social entrepreneurship has changed through the years. Early in the twentieth century, people like Nelson Rockefeller and J.P. Morgan were seen as great entrepreneurs who reached out to society by establishing large businesses. More recently it has been the Jimmy Carters, Mark Zuckerbergs, Bill Clintons, and Bill Gateses who have assumed that role in less ostentatious, yet enormously helpful, ways. Nevertheless, they, too, are well-known figures to the public at large.

Many of today's social entrepreneurs are a different breed. Most are unknowns who have taken back projections onto powerful figures and experts, and are using their own power and authority to address the world's needs. *Entrepreneur* can refer to the most ordinary of citizens.

Pat Kneisler, an antiwar protester, stepped up to the plate when the U.S. Department of Defense's tally of U.S. casualties in Iraq frustrated many Americans. The numbers on its website were updated slowly and showed different fatality counts from those in the media. Kneisler posted her own self-researched tally of troop casualties on the web to show what she considered a more accurate count.

One entrepreneur developed NanoLab, a handheld lab for areas where medical lab equipment is not available. A few graduate students promoted a low-cost baby incubator through a video on YouTube. A single college student developed Orphans Against AIDS, which pays for schooling for children affected by AIDS in poor countries. While still in college, another student collected old reading glasses and shipped them to poor countries. Within a few years, her organization, Unite for Sight, had provided eye care for 200,000 people.

An insightful reader of the *San Jose Mercury News* took matters into her own hands and wrote the following letter to the editor: "Unless somebody wakes up and looks at the real problem, we are doomed to fail. The world's population is doubling every 50 years, and if our efforts to reduce carbon-dioxide emissions by 50 percent are successful, 50 years from now we will be back at square one. [We must] persuade the world's population that they must start working to slow its growth."

Wangari Maathai, who was awarded the 2004 Nobel Peace Prize for founding a movement that planted 30 million trees in Kenya and throughout Africa, inspired citizens of a depressed area in Northern California to plant a minimum of ten trees for each person living in their town.

These are a sampling of individual entrepreneurs who have engaged their inner authority, passion, and unique gifts in reaching out to address the world's needs.

COLLECTIVE USE OF INDIVIDUAL AUTHORITY

A highly visible sign of inner authority and power rising within the average person played out in the streets of the Middle East and North Africa.

When hundreds of thousands of Iranians marched silently through the streets of Tehran, protesting the disputed presidential election, the government quelled their demonstrations. However, the protests merely shifted online, where tech-savvy Iranians tweeted pictures and messages to the world in real time as events unfolded. At the same time, hackers targeted web pages of Iran's leadership, demanding Internet freedom. To protect the activists, a website called NedaNet was launched, providing a system of proxy sites to cloak the location of users in Iran from the Iranian government. In turn, a San Franciscan assisted the Iranian techies by launching Haystack, a program to help them wiggle past government filters. Each step of the way, individuals saw a need and brought their own particular abilities to the protest, helping one another in whatever way they could.

More recently an outbreak of demonstrations in the Arab world went viral. Individuals across Tunisia, Egypt, Libya, Yemen, Bahrain, and Syria took to the streets in peaceful protest of their repressive regimes, with success in several of them—at least for now. "In just a few months, ordinary people across the region—ordinary in everything but their courage—have upended decades of expert assurances that Arabs would never rebel against their dreadful dictators."[lii] Those experts never encountered the surging energy in ordinary citizens who are connected with their inner authority and power.

All generations have engaged in demonstrations, but gatherings of these courageous individuals have a different formation. They are not groups coming together, but individuals without a leader, linking their inner authority with that of others to exert common power. They are informed through the Internet and have chosen to express their own concerns. These are average, everyday citizens making a difference to society in ways that are in keeping with their personality, interests, gifts, and capabilities. A measure of their effectiveness is governmental censorship, which expanded from four countries in 2002 to forty in 2010.

Energy from within these individuals rose up in defense of their rights, and they acted accordingly with authority and power. Although their minds were on the task at hand, they were actually doing much more: they were living their part in raising consciousness to a higher level.

THE SIGNIFICANCE FOR SOULF

One of the most energetic movements of soulf in the world today is the emergence of the average person in shaping the course of human history and consciousness. People are finding the world inside themselves, where they can envision the transformation needed by the universe. Some individuals are already moved to carry their unique vision into the world. Others will join them with their own vision as memes spread, encouraging individuals to live out the deepest needs of the universe.

7

Regressive Energy

Most individuals desire positive transformation in the world, but some feel more closely connected to negative energy. This phenomenon exists throughout creation. A magnet's negative energy counteracts its positive energy, gravity tempers expansion of the universe, and dark matter tames dark energy. Similarly, regressive energy strikes back at progressive energy at humanity's level, which is halfway between the macroworld and the microworld.

Any evolutionary thrust needs both positive and negative energy to pull in opposite directions—balanced in favor of the positive—to provide grist for propelling the movement forward. Accordingly, the cosmic energy engaged in drawing humanity together, whether through the Internet, in developing robots, in dissolving boundaries, or in releasing the inner power of the individual, also has actualized negative forms.

CYBER WARFARE

Balancing the many positive uses of the Internet to cohere humanity is its use to attack another country, which separates people. The Pentagon considers cyberspace a war-fighting domain, and President Obama has declared that cyber attacks on the United States could be considered an act of war.

Every day, organized criminals and hackers from various nations, including Russia and China, launch thousands of attacks on federal and private computer systems in the United States. The Pentagon has employed thousands of young computer geeks (hacker soldiers) to address the situation, blending new technologies into U.S.

war planning. The juxtaposition of the Pentagon and young computer geeks boggles the mind:

> "Rock music blares and empty cans of Mountain Dew pile up as engineers create tools to protect the Pentagon's computers and crack into the networks of countries that could become adversaries. Prizes like cappuccino machines and stacks of cash spur them on, and a gong heralds each major breakthrough."[liii]

The danger of cyber warfare is of utmost concern to the federal government. An espionage expert wrote: "[At the White House] the Situation Room's biggest nightmare is cyberwar—electronic malware that would penetrate to the inner lobes of the national security brain."[liv] Terrorists could sit with a keyboard and remotely shut down factory assembly lines or devastate cities by opening a dam's floodgates. China's intelligence agencies could embed a malicious code in Chinese-made computer chips, enabling them to take command of U.S. computers by remote control over the Internet.

Already, international hackers have withdrawn $9 million from 2,100 ATM terminals in 280 cities across the globe in twelve hours. Although cyber warfare would not be as deadly as atomic war, cyber attacks "with the ability to threaten the U.S. money supply is the equivalent of today's nuclear weapon," said a former director[lv] of U.S. national intelligence.

ROBOTS

Though some boundaries are broken down through the use of robots, others are erected through their use in war. Robots operate machine guns and explode improvised explosive devices (IEDs) in combat zones. Predator drones, pilotless aerial vehicles, collect intelligence and conduct bombing raids in Pakistan. Robots have been so effective that the Pentagon has set 2015 as the deadline for one-third of its ground combat vehicles to be unmanned, self-thinking machines that can fight in war zones. However, ethical and safety questions about the use of robots are holding back any rush to use them extensively in fighting future wars. Because they are so effective, even plugging themselves in when they need a charge, there is danger they could take over their own decision making.

TERRORISTS

As energy rises in most of humanity to fulfill the individual and benefit the world, some individuals are using their newfound authority and power for destructive purposes. Terrorists are of grave concern internationally.

Terrorists present a new and different kind of challenge for governments worldwide, whose armed forces were designed for warfare between two highly consolidated and structured armies. The enemies of the United States today are "very decentralized, very networked . . . They're sort of the eBay of terrorism."[lvi]

Mumbai

A prime example is the terrorist attack on the global financial capital of India. A group of terrorists attacked a luxury hotel in Mumbai and a Jewish travelers' center run by an ultra-orthodox sect, leaving 166 people dead and 300 injured. Their ability to spread terror was largely increased by the use of the Internet and other advanced technology, which linked them in real time with Pakistan-based handlers.

Suicide Bombers

Suicide bombs are a direct form of using personal inner authority and power for destructive purposes. Observing no national boundaries, 658 suicide bombers made attacks around the world in a single year. "Increasingly, we are seeing the globalization of suicide bombs, no longer confined to conflict zones but happening anywhere . . .[Suicide bombers are] martyrs without borders."[lvii]

Masks

Another problem for traditional armies is the use of masks, which were used by both the fighters of Hamas and Fatah in the Palestinian civil war in Gaza:

> "These masks are the uniforms of the new armies of the 21st century and the new kind of violence, [which] no longer distinguishes between war against the stranger and war against members of your own society . . . this new violence doesn't

have a front, it doesn't have a face. It doesn't have boundaries.

These young men do not report to anyone above them. They have no ranks. No leader can ever be sure of their allegiance. Every masked man is a general, and every militia is a cross between a self-funded criminal gang and a modern army . . . You can expect to see a lot more confrontations between armies in uniforms and helmets and armies in blue jeans and masks."[lviii]

The fact that no leader can be sure of their allegiance has caused a major problem for the United States in Afghanistan and Pakistan. Figuring out where loyalties of the Taliban and al-Qaeda lie is like a shell game, always shifting, never sure.

THE SIGNIFICANCE FOR SOULF

An incorrect assumption is that negative energy can be eradicated. Until we move beyond this way of thinking, we will continue to be shocked when we hear of another suicide bombing or computer attack, and we will struggle—unsuccessfully—to wipe out that evil! Each time we think we have killed it, another form pops up with more virulent energy.

We need to accept that regressive energy is here to stay, as part of the composition of the world, and learn new modes of working with it. Negative energy must be reunited with the positive energy from which it has become cut off. Only at that higher level can we bring to a standstill the many-headed Hydra we keep feeding, and experience the peace we so desire.

CHAPTER

8

Balancing the Eastern and Western Worlds

With the world drawing closer together and boundaries between individuals and nations beginning to fade, a layer of unbalanced relationships has surfaced. In order for humanity to become one people in one world, these relationships need to transform.

One form of imbalance glares openly: imbalance between the East and West.

EASTERN COUNTRIES

Jet Airways ran a full-page ad in a California newspaper that subtly, or not so subtly, suggested the encroachment of Asian countries on the global status of the United States. The ad featured a black page with a modest white caption in the top half that read, "India is about to get closer."

In 2010, India and China were already the two fastest-growing of the G-20 countries. Regional markets were opening up, and these two were poised to take advantage of the situation. China had secured the number two position in a list of the world's largest economies, with the United States still number one and Japan taking the number three spot. In 2011, the United States held a 22 percent share of the world's gross domestic product (GDP), but economists predict by 2030 China will account for 19 percent of world GDP, leaving the United States behind at 16 percent.

With the developing trend of regional markets, Hong Kong became a world center for floating new stock listings, surging past New York to become number two in the world for launching initial public offerings (IPOs).

London maintained its number one position and New York fell to number three.

Perhaps a harbinger of the power shift from West to East is the influx of Southeast Asian immigrants to the United States. Until the mid-twentieth century, immigrants to America came, for the most part, from Southern and Eastern Europe. Since then, Congress has opened up U.S. immigration policy, welcoming people from other parts of the world. Many of these newer immigrants have been Southeast Asians. The Asian population in California surged even during the recent economic downturn, rising to comprise almost a third of the state's population. Following close behind the immigrant rush is an explosion of imports from Thailand, South Korea, Taiwan, and Japan.

The East is, indeed, getting closer. Japanese car sales in California surpassed domestic models, grabbing nearly half of the California market. Biotech experts in Silicon Valley are being lured to India and China. Even as biotech firms in Northern California were on the cusp of a commercial explosion, with 300 medical products on the market and nearly 400 more in late-stage tests, biotech experts saw the writing on the wall: "We are starting to see part of a 'brain drain' of biotech talent heading to China, India and other nations where it is cheaper to operate with fewer government regulations. That is what's alarming," warned a venture partner with an investment firm.[lix]

In India, hitherto unknown companies, such as TataMotors, joined the big boys in buying out other companies to become more competitive. Flexing its muscles as a fledgling international economic player, TataMotors bought Jaguar and Land Rover from Ford Motor. "[India has] developed the technology and ability to become world-class car manufacturers," commented a director of The Global Network of Entrepreneurs.[lx]

By 2011, India's outsourcing strategy had taken a dramatic turn. The anticipated brain drain had turned into a torrent. Instead of gathering large numbers of cheap engineers in India to be the help desk for the United States, India began hiring thousands of costly engineers in Silicon Valley to help India's economic march.

As a final blow to American self-esteem, foreign countries started winning disputes in U.S. courts. One of the largest claimants, a Hong Kong conglomerate, won a $2.8 billion judgment against a company that provides interactive video technology. All boundaries had been broken; world relationships were becoming balanced.

According to a survey conducted by the Consumer Electronics Association, eight in ten Americans said the United States would lose its innovation advantage in the global economy over the next decade, while close to half believed Japan or China had already surpassed the United States in innovation. "Forty-three percent said remaining the world's innovation leader was the most important factor for future U.S. successes, ranking higher than economic size or military supremacy."[lxi] If the 43 percent are right, where does that leave the United States?

CHINA

With developing consciousness, Americans began to see their own country more realistically in relation to the rest of the world. They observed the scales tipping toward the East in terms of world prominence and power, and saw that China had become a major player on the world scene. What the rest of the world had recognized for some time, Americans could no longer deny: as the United States struggles to stay number one in the world, China is rising in world stature, overshadowing the spotlight on the United States. At the rate it is changing and growing, China will overtake the United States as front-runner in the world by the middle of the twenty-first century.

A sure sign of this new consciousness is the demand for learning Chinese in the United States. As of 2010, Chinese was the third most-tested advanced placement language on college board exams. Although this interest probably derived from the business and trade world, it is nonetheless significant that the next generation see China as a major world partner in their future.

China's business and trade are flourishing. China is Intel's second-largest consumer market after the United States, and U.S. imports from China increased 101 percent between 2000 and 2005. China overtook the United States in car sales and is the world's most populous mobile phone market. Even more worrisome to the United States is Hong Kong's rank as second in the world for launching IPOs, a fact that supports the belief of nearly half of Americans that China has already surpassed the United States in innovation.

Internally, China has also undergone significant change. It is experiencing the biggest migration of people from rural to urban centers in global history, while its illiteracy rate has dropped significantly below that for developing countries as a whole.

One-ninth of China's energy needs are now met by hydropower generated by the Three Gorges Dam, which was designed to produce energy equivalent to the output of eighteen coal or nuclear power plants and to increase China's shipping volume 400 percent.

Perhaps the most significant choice of direction for China has been its Green Revolution, seen by Thomas Friedman of *The New York Times* as the most important thing to happen in the first decade of the twenty-first century.[lxii] China became aware that green energy technology is both a necessity and an opportunity. The volume of wind, solar, mass transit, nuclear, and more efficient coal-burning projects launched by China in 2009 is, in itself, stunning.

According to a survey in 2008, the people of China are more satisfied than people of any other nation. Eighty-six percent were content with their country's direction, and 82 percent were satisfied with their national economy.[lxiii]

With confidence, a new China is now willing to reach out to the world, symbolized by the Beijing Olympics Bird's Nest and its cutting-edge architecture. Internal development, trade, and outreach to the rest of the world have made it one of the two fastest growing of the G-20 countries, with the third largest economy in the world. Dollars that spell "higher debt" to Americans read "higher earnings" to the Chinese. In 2010, the World Economic Forum even questioned whether a Beijing Consensus would replace the Washington Consensus.[lxiv]

A political commentator said, "An end of America's pre-eminence as the world's foremost industrial and technological power. An end to the Second American Century, as the Asian Century begins."[lxv]

THE SIGNIFICANCE FOR SOULF

What we have just witnessed are overt signs of soulf's energizing the Eastern half of the world. However, invisible signs are more significant in understanding what lies behind soulf's movement.

An unseen meridian divides the eastern and western hemispheres of the globe. As people in opposite hemispheres, we are opposites in many ways.

Westerners tend to be more extraverted; are faster paced in living; and place higher value on accomplishments, doing, staying active, and making clear, rational decisions. Easterners tend to value introspection, irrational ways of being, wholeness, entering into the flow of life, and letting life happen.

It could be said that the culture of the West favors the left half of the brain, whereas culture in the East favors the right hemisphere. The left side of the brain is the verbal, rational, and decision-making side. The right half is the artistic, irrational, and holistic side.

Easterners and Westerners together form humanity's brain. Humanity has reached a point where its left brain hemisphere has tipped the scales too far and needs to be balanced by its right brain.

Certain functions of the right brain are especially needed at this time, in both the East and West, to handle evolving situations in the world:

- *Nonverbal ideation* for innovations of a new kind

- *Spatial orientation* to balance the out-of-control time orientation of the Western world

- *Sense of pattern* for seeing the patterning of the universe, so humanity can better cooperate with it

- *Intuitive problem solving* for problems that lie beyond rational thinking

- *Psychic experiences* for connecting with the unconscious and other abstract levels of reality

- *Simultaneous processing* for multitasking in a more efficient, less hectic, holistic way

These functions underlie soulf's dramatic move to energize the right hemisphere of humanity's brain, which can be enabled most effectively by energizing the Eastern hemisphere of the world.

CHAPTER

9

Balancing Humanity and The Natural World

Humanity has struck an imbalance with the environment at the point of global warming, so now it must help the universal body as it struggles to heal itself. Humanity, too, is entangled in the fallout from the imbalance because *homo sapiens* is an intrinsic part of the natural world. There is no escape.

Dawning consciousness of this reality brought humanity to greater concern and action following the release of Al Gore's film, "An Inconvenient Truth." Scientists had been aware of global warming for decades prior to the film, but a reluctant humanity kept denying it.

At an energy conference sponsored by *Newsweek*, a physicist underscored the imminent threat we face: "'Earth is like the great ship Titanic,' on a collision course with disaster unless action is taken. 'Off in the distance is an iceberg, so how do you turn the ship so there is only a glancing blow? . . . And the good ship Earth takes time to turn.'"[lxvi]

GREENING THE ENVIRONMENT

Greening the environment became a cool thing to endorse, as if the floodgates of political correctness had suddenly burst open. Even major oil companies felt the need to hop aboard the bandwagon. Chevron took a bold stance with environmentalists and kept advertising "We agree!" A green movement coalesced and spread around the Earth to heal humanity's relationship with the natural world. The universe had found a course of least resistance to restore the health of Planet Earth.

At least it had a foot in the door. Despite incontrovertible evidence, significant numbers of people still drag their feet when it comes to facing the inconvenient truth. Regressive energy is always reluctant to let go.

"I think that the most important thing to happen this past year was that living and thinking 'green'—that is, mobilizing for the environmental/energy challenge we now face— hit Main Street." — Thomas L. Friedman[lxvii]

Cars and Trucks

Focal point for much of the greening effort has been the powering of vehicles. Following up on the first federal regulations of fuel efficiency and greenhouse gas emissions in cars and light trucks, President Obama announced mileage and pollution limits for commercial trucks and buses, as well.

Battery technology improved to the point where plug-in hybrid electric vehicles may well supplant gasoline-guzzling cars. They are dramatically cheaper to operate, consuming about two cents' worth of electricity to travel one mile, compared with the current cost of twenty to twenty-five cents per mile for gasoline.

McDonald's started featuring free electric car charging stations at one of its North Carolina restaurants. If the venture in Raleigh proved successful, the company planned to add charging stations at restaurants in other locations. Nova Charge, distributor of the ChargePoint stations, has distributed hundreds of units in the United States at a manufacturing cost of $5,000 apiece.

Another idea for reduction of hydrocarbons is car sharing, which reduces the need for individual cars. Zipcar, a car-sharing company, enlists many college campuses nationwide into their green-friendly program, as well as reaching out to the public at large. Zipcars are available around the clock for an annual fee of $35, plus $8 or $9 an hour. The concept of car sharing seems to be catching on, as Zipcars are showing up on streets and at shopping centers across the country in increasing numbers.

Energy-Efficient Lighting

A greening strategy for the average household has been the switch to energy-efficient lighting. A coalition of private companies and government agencies[lxviii] launched a marketing campaign, 18Seconds, luring Americans to replace incandescent bulbs with compact fluorescent ones, which are more energy efficient and last longer.

"If every American swapped just one lightbulb for an ENERGY STAR labeled CFL or LED bulb, it would collectively save more than $8 billion in energy costs and remove 2 million cars' worth of greenhouse gas emissions from our atmosphere."[lxix]

Environmentalists

Environmentalists continue to prod and support efforts to heal the natural world, bringing ingenious ideas into play to reach their goal.

A fresh idea came from Environmental Defense and Natural Resources Defense Council (NRDC). Two big buyout firms wanted to buy TXU, a giant Texas utility, but they did not want to become embroiled in a war with environmentalists over a plan to build eleven coal-fired power plants. They told Fred Krupp, president of Environmental Defense: "We only want to go forward if you and NRDC will praise what we are trying to do here."[lxx]

After negotiations with the environmentalists, the private equity group finally agreed to reduce the number of coal plants from eleven to three, to support a U.S. cap on greenhouse gas emissions, to invest $400 million in energy-efficient programs at TXU, and to double its wind power.

Krupp insightfully remarked,

"What is the message when the largest buyout in history is made contingent (by the buyers) on winning praise for its greenhouse gas plan? The markets are ahead of the politicians. The world has changed, and these guys see it . . . Going online, we shifted this from a local debate over generating electricity to a national debate over capping and reducing greenhouse gas emissions."[lxxi]

Investments in Clean Tech

With the surge of interest in going green, global investment in clean technology gained momentum.

In 2007, Silicon Valley venture firms invested $1 billion in the energy sector of the economy, setting a new record: the $1 billion investment in clean tech in that single year equaled the combined amount invested in clean tech from 2000 to 2005. Venture capital investments in international clean tech surged to nearly $2 billion in the first quarter of 2010, a new quarterly record.

In earlier days, clean-tech investment focused primarily on solar power and biofuels, but in recent years the field has broadened and become more diverse. China and Europe dominate the solar and wind markets, and Brazil the alternative fuel market, but vast opportunities still exist for more players. In fact, a major company that does not have a green component today is an exception to the rule and may find itself left behind in the dust.

Involvement of Businesses

Wal-Mart developed an eco-rating system for hundreds of thousands of its products and experimented with alternative building materials, lighting, power systems, and designs in two new green stores. Many suppliers of Wal-Mart have taken steps to become more eco-friendly. For example, Levi Strauss now recommends its jeans be washed in warm or cold water, as opposed to hot water, which uses more energy.

Wal-Mart launched a massive campaign about the benefits of compact fluorescent light bulbs (CFLs) and devoted significant floor space in each store to educate consumers. The company saw that even though the bulbs would pay for themselves in a short time, the upfront cost was about twelve times that of incandescent bulbs, more than people were willing to pay. So Wal-Mart successfully negotiated with General Electric to lower its price of CFLs by 21 percent.

An op-ed piece commented, "The more energy-saving bulbs Wal-Mart sells, the more innovation it triggers, the more prices go down. That's how you get scale. And scale is everything if you want to change the world."[lxxii]

New Resource Bank was the first commercial bank to be founded with the purpose of loaning money to businesses developing environmentally friendly products. In addition, the bank reaches out to depositors who want their money used for projects that create jobs and profits by reducing global warming. Its building in San Francisco is gold certified under green building standards, and the bank offers up to $60 a week to employees to take public transit.

Cisco Systems collaborated with an organization called Metropolis, a group of 106 large cities (mostly outside the United States) to help leaders use technology to be more efficient and less polluting. This step took Cisco beyond its core products of routers and switches to develop smart sensors, technology that automatically adjusts lighting and air conditioning according to the times of actual use. Smart sensors are now used in public buildings and private offices, as well as in residences, to monitor the efficiency of energy use.

Even as the housing market was crashing during the recent recession, developer Warmington Homes built a cluster of environmentally friendly townhomes with a range of standard water- and energy-efficient features, from solar panels to very low flush toilets, drought-resistant landscaping, and tankless water heaters. These homes

104

proved to be so popular the developer was able to increase the initial offering price.

Involvement of Governments

All levels of government became involved in the green movement, and venture capital investment in international clean tech surged.

At the city level, Washington, D.C. started requiring private buildings, in addition to government buildings, to be certified as green. The U.S. Energy Secretary[lxxiii] pointed out that merely the inclusion of smart sensors could reduce energy consumption in office buildings by 80 percent.

Not waiting for federal legislation, California's governor[lxxiv] enacted several pieces of legislation to address global warming. A major law, California Global Warming Solutions Act, mandated the state's reduction of greenhouse-gas emissions to 1990 levels by 2020. The legislation fundamentally changed the consumption of energy, lessened dependency on foreign oil and reduced greenhouse-gas emissions. The governor also joined with the British prime minister[lxxv] in sharing clean-energy technology.

The U.S. federal government finally came through with funding for technology in the American Recovery and Reinvestment Act, which now gives tax credits for advanced energy manufacturing.

The United Arab Emirates (UAE) launched the Masdar Initiative, which seeks to reduce demand on fossil fuels internationally by making the UAE a center for the development and implementation of clean-energy technology. As the fourth largest oil producer in the Organization of the Petroleum Exporting Countries (OPEC), holding about 10 percent of the known resources, the country had previously been named one of the world's highest per capita emitters of greenhouse gases.

Former President Bill Clinton drew a coalition of twenty-two of the world's largest cities into his Clinton Climate Initiative to limit global warming. One project undertaken by the group, called C40 Cities, is designed to reduce emissions in forty cities, each with area populations of three million or more, which together account for 15 to 20 percent of the world's emissions. The international consortium bargains for cheaper energy-efficient products and shares ideas about cutting greenhouse-gas pollution.

Kofi Annan, former Secretary General of the United Nations, is very concerned about carbon emissions. He spent most of his time in office getting companies worldwide to sign on to Global Impact. This agreement set international environmental standards for carbon emissions and other disturbances in eco-systems, such as ballast dumping and infectious diseases borne on jets.

The United Nations' Montreal Protocol, an ozone treaty that eliminated chlorofluorocarbons and replaced them with hydrofluorocarbons (HFCs), was ratified by 195 nations. Recognizing that even HFCs damage the atmosphere, though to a lesser extent, the Obama administration asked the same nations that ratified the Montreal Protocol to enact mandatory reductions in HFCs to totally eliminate ozone-depleting materials.

Each of these means of involvement in greening the environment is an important step in the right direction, but the universe is pushing for the end of global warming *now*. The timeless universe is always in the now, and is goal oriented, but humanity lives in chronological time. Humans must bring rational judgment to the pressing need of the universe and be satisfied temporarily with intermediary energy alternatives.

INTERMEDIARY SOURCES OF ALTERNATIVE ENERGY

Biofuels

Biofuel use began to increase dramatically in 2009. Research funding became more available, and a federal mandate required producers to supply 36 billion gallons of biofuels annually by 2022.

The use of biofuels goes back to the days of Henry Ford, who designed the Model T to run on ethanol or gas. Prohibition ruined his plan because of the basic crop's alcoholic content, but his idea is now resurging.

Corn ethanol, the most common biofuel, is one possibility. Today researchers are experimenting with everything from plant waste or dedicated biofuel crops[lxxvi] to pond algae, pecan shells, and sugar cane.

The key for most ethanol production is a cheap source of sugar, which usually requires breaking down tough cell walls in plants. To address this problem, researchers at the University of California at Berkeley analyzed rumen from cow stomachs, hoping to reverse the process by which bacteria break down plant cell walls, to turn grass into energy.

Algae are an exception to the centrality of sugar in energy production. Though they require the addition of sugar, algae produce more energy than do other biofuels.

With the array of possibilities for biofuel production, the most likely scenario for the future is a smorgasbord of fuels. "We're going to end up with a number of different processes, creating a number of different transportation fuels."[lxxvii]

Biodiesel Fuel

Biodiesel fuel is also coming onstage. The number of diesel manufacturing plants in the United States has more than tripled. Some people are even using cooking oil or used frying grease from restaurants to run their cars. All that is needed is a biodiesel conversion kit, costing about $700 installed.

Cows have shown value for today's energy crisis beyond having their rumen analyzed by scientists. For several years Pacific Gas and Electric Company (PG&E) has been using natural gas from the manure of five thousand cows to create electricity for fifty thousand homes. Dairy farms in Texas and Wisconsin are engaged in similar projects.

Biofuels and biodiesel fuel are useful as intermediaries while seeking to curtail greenhouse gases. Ultimately, however, humanity needs to work within the parameters of natural law to the end-stage of clean, sustainable energy, which will rebalance humanity and the natural world at the point of global warming.

END-STAGE: CLEAN ENERGY

Wind Turbines and Photovoltaics

While the prices of traditional fuels—coal, oil, and gas—have risen dramatically off and on, technology has made a stunning reduction in the cost of wind turbines and of photovoltaics, which converts sunlight into electricity.

Texas has built more than five gigawatts of wind-turbine capacity, representing almost 10 percent of the state's electrical supply. Given the fact that wind energy costs seven cents per kilowatt hour, compared with twelve cents per kilowatt hour to build a gas-fired power plant, Texas's action is not surprising.

The cost of photovoltaics has fallen to an almost marketable level, while retail electricity prices have been increasing by as much as 30 percent. At the price it has reached in New York, a photovoltaic installation on the rooftop of a house will pay for itself in less than ten years, with a greater than 10 percent return on one's capital investment. However, the biggest bang for the buck lies in the fact that both solar and wind energy generate absolutely no greenhouse gases.

Solar Thermal

Some companies are advocating large-scale solar thermal facilities, though environmentalists denounce them. A solar thermal plant consists of rows of gigantic mirrors covering an area bigger than two football fields. They are, in fact, giant boilers made of glass and steel, which use the sun's heat to create steam to power turbines that generate electricity. Though currently costing about eighteen cents a kilowatt hour, improved technology could lower the cost to about five cents a kilowatt hour by 2025. Executives at Ausra, a solar thermal company, say that "a square patch of desert about 92 miles long on each side blanketed with Ausra's technology could generate enough electricity to meet the entire nation's demand."[lxxviii]

California has the largest operating collection of solar thermal facilities in the world, with more on the drawing board. As the world's eighth-largest economy, California has a daunting challenge to provide sources of renewable energy that can transform its electricity system. Some people think solar thermal is a system that could achieve that goal.

Geothermal and Space Solar

Geothermal technology, which taps into earth energy, is an alternative to home heating and cooling systems, saving as much as 70 percent on energy bills. PG&E is pursuing yet another alternative: space solar. Space-solar installations would generate electricity from solar-powered satellites in space. The satellites would use solar cells to convert the sun's energy to electricity, then transmit that power to Earth as radio-frequency energy, which would convert the energy to electricity. The project is expected to deliver 200 megawatts of power[lxxix] to California by 2016.

Nuclear Energy

Nuclear energy is the most controversial of alternative energies. Though it produces less waste than do fossil fuels, its radioactive waste is extremely hazardous. Because of the danger, it is stored in special containers and is usually buried deep inside a mountain.

U.S. power plants produce two thousand metric tons of radioactive waste each year. However, this replaces an estimated 690 million metric tons of carbon dioxide from entering the atmosphere.

Currently nuclear power plants use the nuclear-fission process. Nuclear fusion, which combines atoms into one rather than splitting an atom in two, is potentially safer energy, but nuclear fusion technology has not yet been developed to operate within a large power plant.

THE SIGNIFICANCE FOR SOULF

Wind turbines have sprung up on hilltops, while rows of gigantic mirrors placed in sunny, open spaces set to work as giant boilers to provide solar thermal energy. Experimentation with geothermal, space solar, photovoltaic, and fusion energy is underway. No method of harnessing energy is off the table, though nuclear energy remains highly controversial.

Of necessity, humanity must proceed at a slower pace than the universe is demanding, but it needs to convert to sustainable energy as fast as possible. Creating balance between humanity and the universe at the point of global warming is critical to the health not only of Planet Earth, but also of the universe itself. Remember, the universe is a single, organic, interdependent whole, of which humanity is a part. When the universe is sick, so are we.

CHAPTER

10

Balancing the Seen and Unseen Worlds

"Our main ecological problems, like climate change . . . are linked to our overuse of material energy," says a Jungian analyst and ecologist.[lxxx] Both the material and psychic spheres affect everything, so any imbalance between the two upsets the careful balancing of the universe as a whole. If we have hopes of healing our rift with the universe, we must consider inner and outer nature equally, as both are needed for the transformation of energy.

Energy is the battery of life on Earth and of transformation of matter. All of us desire it, both as psychic energy (inspiration, love, knowledge, etcetera) and as material energy (money, oil, food, etcetera). Our problem is not the use of energy but the consequences of using energy in an unbalanced way.

Energy is central in ecology and psychology. Both disciplines require equal consideration of inner and outer nature to support their transformation. By listening to the symbolic content of a particular problem—inner or outer—we can determine what life needs from humans to transform its energy.

OBESITY

Symbolic Obesity

Looking at the symbolic content of obesity, one sees that it is running wild in the world, far beyond human stomachs. The world's population is doubling every fifty years, crowding out other species and seriously affecting biodiversity. Large corporations have added to their weight by gobbling up smaller companies, like Pac-Man on a spree. Financial institutions that grew too big to fail needed huge bailouts when they encountered obesity's downside. Humanity has made almost suicidal use of material energy, including oil, forests, and other material resources. Excessive consumerism and the mounting debt of governmental bodies are out of control. The massive debt crisis that has resulted hangs like a noose not only around the neck of the United States, but Europe and the world at large. Obesity is taking a heavy toll on humanity and culture.

Human Obesity

Obesity in humans, the form of obesity we know best, is an example of overuse of material energy, causing a serious health problem for our nation. Beginning early in the 1960s, Americans started down the dangerous road of developing an imbalance with their own human nature. The nation gradually gained weight until the 1980s, when stomachs suddenly ballooned. In just ten years Americans had collectively gained more than a billion pounds. "If this was about tuberculosis, it would be called an epidemic."[lxxxi] The trend is pushing the United States toward becoming a nation of obese and overweight people.

"Conditioned hypereating works the same way as other 'stimulus response' disorders in which reward is involved, such as compulsive gambling and substance abuse." — David A. Kessler[lxxxii]

The obesity rate in children and teens has tripled since 1980. Forty percent of young women and 25 percent of young men weigh too much to enlist in the U.S. military.

Obesity has not spared even the newest family members, dogs. Veterinarians say it has reached epidemic proportions in them and appears to be increasing. Five percent of dogs in the United States are obese and another 20 to 30 percent are overweight, making obesity one of their biggest health issues.

Hospitals have had to buy special wheelchairs and operating tables to accommodate the obese; revolving doors have had to be widened; undertakers now offer triple-wide coffins; airlines fork over an extra quarter of a billion dollars annually for jet fuel because of the added weight; and extra pounds carried by Americans add an estimated 90 billion dollars a year to the country's medical spending. "Obesity is inescapably confirming itself as one of the biggest drains" on national health-care budgets worldwide.[lxxxiii]

Newer editions of *Joy of Cooking* have lowered the predicted number of servings for identical recipes from previous editions because our voracious appetites have gone out of control. Jumbo-size boxes of popcorn are promoted at movie theaters, and bagels have grown over the years from 140 calories to 350 calories each.

People judge food amounts on units. They will not buy two boxes of popcorn because that seems greedy, but they will buy a jumbo-size because it is just one. The same is true for fries and Cokes and hamburgers. McDonalds's sodas grew from the original eight ounces to a sixteen-ounce small soda and a thirty-two-ounce (300 calories) large soda. Soft drinks used to be reserved for special occasions, but now they comprise 7 percent of the average American's diet.

However, changes in eating habits have begun to sprout up. First Lady Michelle Obama awakened Americans' consciousness to healthy eating by starting an organic vegetable garden at the White House, and later publishing a cookbook of recipes created in the White House kitchen. She highlighted healthy eating and the health hazard of obesity. This resulted in many restaurants posting nutritional information on their menus and lowering the number of calories in food preparation.

Hospitals, too, are promoting good health with more appealing menus that include locally produced organic foods for inpatients, staff, and administrators, and in their cafeterias for the general public. An obstetrician at Kaiser Permanente Hospitals started a movement to put farmers' markets outside thirty Kaiser hospitals. Some of them are even sprouting onsite organic gardens and raising free-range chickens.

Michael Moore brought the issue of obesity to a head in his pointedly revealing movie, "Super-sized Me," in which he laid out a strong case for the central role fast food plays in the obesity epidemic.

A recent study by the Institute of Medicine suggests that giving toddlers the amount of food they should eat may help curb obesity in the future because two- and three-year-olds are sensitive to portion size. Humanity may be inadvertently training them to overeat by giving them larger portions than their bodies need.

Obesity and Overpopulation

As the number of humans on Earth passes the seven billion mark, obesity in the form of overpopulation is taking a heavy toll. The runaway population growth plays a crucial role in both societal and natural problems: human health, food, clean water, and encroachments on natural habitats through urban sprawl. A population biologist said, "Population and consumption are no more separable in producing environmental damage than the length and width of a rectangle can be separated in producing its area—both are equally important."[lxxxiv]

Galaxies and Obesity

Left without restraint, galaxies would have suffered a similar fate to that of humanity by consuming too many stars, planets and other bits of matter. However, the universe governed its growth with "dark energy, which . . . prevents the biggest clusters of galaxies from getting too fat . . . from essentially overeating."[lxxxv]

Because humanity was created from stardust, we could say humanity has inherited its propensity toward obesity from the natural world but has yet to discover its own form of dark energy to prevent the population from getting too fat.

What is the dark energy that will rebalance the dark matter in humanity and stop it from growing fatter? What will release humanity from too much-ness and enable it to find deeper, healthier satisfaction and balance in the unseen world?

ABSTRACTUALIZATION

The broadest new way of rebalancing matter and energy is through the process of abstractualization; as described in Chapter 1, this refers to abstracting creations from the actualized world and providing a new home for their contents in the unseen world. The life within creations is released from its material form and transformed into a non-material level of existence, leaving the material world less crowded with stuff.

117

Examples of this process have already been noted, without explanation, in Chapter 3, when discussing development of the Internet and electronic devices. One of these processes, texting, abstractualizes communications by abstracting formal language into texting language and digitizing the content. Following is a clever and informative editorial regarding texting language:

"the revenge of e.e. cummings

We had to LOL when we read how txt-msg lingo is replacing stndrd english in student academic pprs. 1 casualty of da trend is uz of capital letter to start a sentence. kids feel free to lowercase everything. pnktu8n is also dissed. tchaz try to help but its often 2 l8.

new paragraphs r not used in txting either. kids prolly think all dis iz ok cuz even Richard Sterling, emeritus xecutiv director of the ntl riting prjct, gives it the nod. natl riting prjct is sposd 2 improve riting instruxn in america's schoolz.

'I think in the future, capitalization will disappear,' he sed in the nytimes. 4 lazy students dis is 2G2BT!

a big natl study by the College Board and Pew Project on the Internet and American Life finds teenagers riting more b/c of txting but in a hybrid language with conventions of its own: call it Textlish. they don't consider it frml english but 64 percent admit it seeps into their writing at school.

we get da need for shorthand when thumbs fly on tiny keypads. but we thot technology wd enhance communication, not blur every boundary b/w frml language and slang. and don't even get us started on emoticons!

1 yng friend of rs recently sent us a hand-ritten thank-u note. we were thrilled at 1st but her spelling wuz awful b/c deres no spellcheck for pen and ppr. same ish w/ txting. ppl get uzd 2 slang and 4get the real words. btw, all of us w/ email addresses r guilty 2, since email usernames r all lowercase and include many weird squiggles. somehow, tho, gnr8ns of secys managed to transl8 Gregg or Pitman shorthand squiggles n2 grammatically correct correspondence 4 their bosses.

well, tempora quid faciunt. Dis not lingo but latin: times change. early america's founders wud uppercase almost every noun; maybe Sterling really is a visionary. Still, on the 25th anniversary of "A Nation at Risk," the seminal report on America's educational challenges, who wudda thot the big threat to riting wd b the cellfone?"[lxxxvi]

Information is abstractualized into cyberspace. Books, magazines, CDs, newspapers, mailboxes, post offices, music stores, book stores, telephone booths, voting booths, maps, heavy cameras, desktop computers—all increasingly have been left behind as the life within them, their real value to the universe, has been digitized.

Abstractualizing to the web requires Internet users to work with abstracted material—something real from everyday life, but in abstracted form. That ability is also necessary for digesting Religion and Mythology within ourselves because we must be able to accept those concepts as abstractions. The attractiveness of the Internet may pave the way for this to happen more easily throughout humanity.

Politics

A prime example of abstractualization is the political process designed by Americans Elect, a new political party. Originally the process for electing political candidates in the United States revolved largely around whistle stops, during which a presidential candidate would make the rounds of clusters of people at train stops. When television became available, people could watch candidates at these whistle stops and could even witness political conventions on TV.

With the digital revolution, things progressed well beyond that. The 2008 presidential election invited questions to presidential candidates from average citizens, who submitted them via video. Average citizens also clustered together on the Internet, bundling contributions in support of political candidates, and some political candidates even held town meetings in Second Life.

Now the political process is jumping into the twenty-first century as Americans Elect uses the newest communication technology to the max. Briefly, its website invites average citizens to prioritize issues and answer specific questions about their stance on them. Choices are matched with a list of possible candidates, nominated by average citizens, from which six are chosen for its online primary.

120

This process transforms the whole political process and carries it to a new level of consciousness. Americans Elect has taken the actualized electoral process, abstracted it, and digitized it. By digitizing the process, it has preserved the original hope of the Constitution makers. The process of selecting a political candidate has become a direct choice of the people, a Jeffersonian style of democracy.[lxxxvii]

As we know, whenever consciousness moves to a higher level, it leaves nothing behind. Contents of former levels are always dissolved into the new form. This is especially obvious in the case of Americans Elect, which is breathing new life into the political process of the Massachusetts town meeting of early America, and seemingly crafting a more perfect union in the process. This could be democracy at its finest.

Work

Although the most pervasive example of abstractualization is digitizing into cyberspace, other areas of living manifest a similar process, especially in work life.

The recent recession triggered the closing of stores and factories and the loss of millions of jobs. Joblessness was exacerbated by more people entering into a do-it-yourself mindset, doing everything from home projects to pumping their own gas to using ATM machines instead of tellers to ordering purchases online instead of shopping in real stores.

More significant for the universe, a widespread abstractualization of work was taking place in the form of tasks becoming digitized (which requires fewer, but more highly educated, workers) and robots performing more tasks. A huge makeover was happening.

In the past, technological innovations and the kinds of jobs they led to were largely in the mechanical realm. Many, perhaps most, of those jobs have disappeared and are never going to return. Too much water has gone over the dam that separates the past from the present needs of the world. Work has shifted toward digitized jobs.

Today innovation itself is abstractualized, as new technology increasingly tilts toward invisible properties. Service technologies, scientific processes, and other abstract-oriented enterprises have taken center stage, easing many mechanical inventions to the wings. Manifestation of this shift is evident in the increasing number of lawsuits involving intellectual property among Silicon Valley companies.

Robots and other automated services are relieving humanity of manual tasks, thus freeing humanity for its primary work of developing higher consciousness. The universe needs individuals to engage life in ways that use their unique gifts and abilities to fulfill their personalities. To the pragmatic universe, fulfillment of humanity's task trumps the job losses incurred and propels humanity into designing novel ways of meeting the new challenge.

Preparation for this change began when loyalty to the workplace dissolved. People began migrating toward freedom of time and space in their work life. They opted for telecommuting, consulting, and jobs that would accompany them and their laptop to wherever they chose to be. They continue to look for ways to abstractualize work and free themselves from the material world. All this has been in (unconscious) service to the universe by rebalancing corporate needs with the needs of the individual for actualizing inner potential.

Corporations have chosen a similar path, releasing companies from the limitations of time and space. Some businesses automate their corporate data centers, a method Hewlett Packard used to cut costs in the sluggish economy. Customer service is increasingly handed over to automation. Companies outsource and offshore work to people in other countries, keep records in the cloud, and hold international conferences in real time via Skype or Second Life, while online sales continue to grow rapidly every year. Abstractualization is the name of the current game.

THE SIGNIFICANCE FOR SOULF

When our attention is constantly grabbed by needs in the material world of everyday living, we may feel uncomfortable with abstractualization and the need to balance the seen and unseen worlds. Yet abstractualization is happening, like it or not. And we have seen the havoc that results from an imbalance between the seen and unseen worlds. Humanity needs to enter the flow of deeper life in an unseen world and move with it. A group that can help us learn how to do this is the Millennial generation.

11

Millennial Generation (Gen Y)

The strongest energy of the universe, at any time in history, is invested in the newest generation. They carry the latest genes into the world, are fresh to the world scene, and exhibit greater malleability than do older generations. They are open to what is, instead of to what has been; are responsive to the energy rising within them; and are eager to live the fullness of life.

The Millennials are no exception. But they have something more to offer. They are becoming adults at the same time that humanity itself is entering adulthood. This combination makes it possible for them to live more mature lives than has generally been the case in the past, and to carry humanity to a higher level of consciousness. They came into the world prepared for that task and are already living into a new consciousness.

In addition, they entered the scene at the turn of the millennium, when life moved into the Aquarian Age, the age of communication. Amazing strides in communications technology were taking place, making their generation the first to be raised with an innate sense of cyberspace and with the Internet as an integral part of their lives.

No other generation can fully understand what it is like to be in their shoes because their psyche has been shaped by an electronic world. At least one neuroscientist believes that "society's growing reliance on technology is likely helping to 'rewire' our brains in ways that are not fully understood."[lxxxviii] The brains of Gen Y, who have spent their entire lives with electronic technology, may already have become rewired. If so, their brains likely have greater plasticity than the brains of older generations.

This would feed into their predisposition to move in new directions of energy flow, making them the most important carriers of life's forward movement today, in terms of the needs of the universe. Only their generation has the particular viewpoint, innate wisdom, life experience, and aptitude to guide the world in the direction it should move in this time of history. Their living is testimony to the universal energy moving in the world today to connect and cohere humanity, and to heal imbalances in the world.

Many imbalances in the world are a non-issue for GenY in their everyday interactions because Millennials accept gays and lesbians, racial differences (40 percent of Millennials are non-white), and diverse cultural practices as a no-brainer. Raised with ecological consciousness, they have respect for and regard themselves as part of the environment. It's just the way life is, and they know they must cooperate with it.

Millennials take to the universe's need for bonding of humanity as a duck takes to water. Facebook, texting, and other social media keep them connected to a wide community of people around the clock and around the world, providing venues for self-expression and relationship. These opportunities reinforce the emergence of the average person and the breaking of boundaries between themselves and the world.

Millennials want immediate access to information along with the latest container for it. They are first to move ahead with newer and faster gadgets, leaving behind slower-paced innovations of the past. When adults were flocking to e-mail in 2006, members of the younger generation were turned off by it because it was too slow. They moved on to instant messaging and posting messages on MySpace, and then shifted to Facebook and to smartphones, texting, iPads, and beyond. As newer, faster forms of digital communication come on the scene, Millennials are there to welcome them.

They feel no need to have information in material form or within themselves. With information so readily available on the Internet, why bother holding it in your head? This viewpoint makes much schoolwork seem as archaic as a slide rule or spelling bees, when one can have the reliability of calculations and spell check at one's fingertips.

Millennials show a particular aptitude for responding to the increased pace of living and to speed in general. They were prepared for this early in life with busily scheduled days, going from soccer practice to music lessons to Boy Scouts, not to mention hours of homework sandwiched in between, or after hours.

They sense intuitively the importance of speed in handling today's complexities and practice it continually through multitasking. They routinely juggle an incoming text from a friend, munching on a handful of chips, keeping their eye on a video, checking their Facebook page—oh yes, and doing homework.

As exasperating as this may be for parents, it furthers the child's experience in dealing with complexities. Millennials have developed their own shorthand language for texting and thrive on the competitive speed of computer games. Their genetic makeup, the environment in which they were raised, and their brain structuring have programmed them to respond in these unfamiliar ways, which match the needs of the universe in regard to today's technological developments.

Millennials have been endowed with a sense of the individual's inner authority, and they are eager to exercise it. Some adults scoff at their audacity, seeing it as a sense of entitlement, but this may be the way Millennials are learning to use their authority and power. It is a needed skill for our time, and trial and error may be the only way they can learn it. No longer do experts and officials hold sway over them because they are living out the potential of becoming their own saviors. When Millennials need advice and support, they turn to each other, not to experts.

Their boldness in exercising authority has contributed greatly to the movement toward a more egalitarian network of power. A mere glance at uprisings in the Arab Spring confirms this. It has followed the universal process of opposites clashing and jumping to a higher level of consciousness.

In this case, individuals have chosen to join with individuals who hold a common desire, and they have confronted those holding an opposite desire with their united power as individuals in community. This is different from uprisings of the past, in which a group or groups came together and exerted their common power. Humanity is beginning to act out a new, higher level of consciousness of innate authority and power, which has been awaiting its full expression in actuality.

Perhaps humanity is now ready to exercise the innate power vested within each individual rather than searching outside for saviors: religious figures, presidents, or other charismatic figures. The self-concern of the Millennial generation may be the start of humanity's taking back into itself the authority that has always resided there but has been projected onto others.

Have we been too afraid to use the awesome power within each one of us? Could the Millennial generation's audacity be soulf's way of driving humanity to claim its own power, so it can become what the universe needs it to be? Is this the beginning of a restructuring of humanity into an ever-widening circle of authority, rather than a hierarchical structure of projected authority? Is soulf drawing people together to live consciously as one world, which, in fact, it already is?

Millennials are uniquely equipped to respond yes to these questions and to move into the future embracing the myriad changes as they happen. This challenges the rest of humanity to act counter-intuitively, bucking the age-old belief that the greatest wisdom necessarily resides in the oldest generation. To be sure, those who have experienced the most of life for the longest time make an important contribution in passing on the wisdom they have gleaned and in connecting the world with its past. But the world also needs to recognize and respect the special wisdom the newest generation is bringing to society, take them seriously, and work cooperatively with them. As life continues to evolve in new directions, it will happen increasingly through the Millennial generation.

An unabridged, unedited manuscript entitled **Where in the World is God?** *includes all the data, notes and references to original sources collected for this study. It is available (free) at:*

https://www.smashwords.com/books/view/262089

Acknowledgments

I want to acknowledge the many individuals and groups of people—named and unnamed—who, in their own unique ways, contributed far more than they suspect in giving birth to this book. Profound thanks to them all!

– The countless individuals, unknown to me personally, who lived the stories of this book through their actions, words, and ideas.

– The numerous newspapers, news services, journalists, and editors who recorded those stories, providing data for this book.

– Jude Berman, my editor, whose intuition, knowledge, and deep insights guided the direction of my writing to its fulfillment.

–John Petroni, who offered unending support and prodding, and elicited insights that enabled me to grow along with the book.

– Betty Howell, for her accompaniment with continuous caring and encouragement throughout the gestation period.

– Steve, who so generously shared his computer expertise and patience in working with his digitally challenged mother.

– Family and friends, for tolerating the long process that kept me from being as present to them as I would have liked.

– And Nikki, who faithfully lay by my side as I wrote, and whose uncanny canine sense knew exactly when I needed to take a break—and insisted I do so!

RESOURCES FOR FURTHER EXPLORATION

Achenbach, Joel, "At the Heart of All Matter: the hunt for the God particle," *National Geographic*, March 2008.

Arntz, William, Betsy Chasse and Mark Vicente, *What the Bleep Do We Know!?* Health Communications, Inc., 2005.

Arntz, William, producer/director, "What the Bleep Do We Know!?" docu-drama, Captured Light Industries, 2006.

Barbour, Ian, *Religion and Science, Historical and Contemporary Issues*, HarperSanFrancisco, 1997.

"Cyberspace and Its Limits: Hypermodern Detours in the Evolution of Consciousness," XXV Annual Gebser Conference, October 1999.

Davies, Paul, *The Fifth Miracle*, Simon and Schuster, 1999.

Dyson, Freeman J., *Infinite In All Directions,* Harper & Row, 1988.

"Evolutionary Timeline", www.talkorigins.org.

Feynman, Richard P., *Six Easy Pieces, Essentials of Physics Explained By Its Most Brilliant Teacher*, Addison-Wesley, 1994.

Gebser, Jean, *The Ever-Present Origin*, (Noel Barstad and Algis Mickunas, translators), Ohio University Press, 1985.

Gibbs, W. Wayt, "Beyond Physics," *Scientific American*, August 1998.

Giegerich, Wolfgang, "The End of Meaning and the Birth of Man," *Journal of Jungian Theory and Practice* (6, no.1), 2004, pp. 1-65.

Giegerich, Wolfgang, *The Soul's Logical Life: Towards a Rigorous Notion of Psychology*, Peter Lang, 2007.

Giegerich, Wolfgang, "Technology and the Soul: From the nuclear bomb to the World Wide Web," Collected English Papers, Vol. II, *Spring* Journal, Inc., pp. 281-308 and 333-336, May 15, 2007.

Gladwell, Malcolm, *The Tipping Point: How Little Things Can Make a Big Difference,* Little, Brown and Company, 2000.

Goodenough, Ursula, *The Sacred Depths of Nature*, Oxford University Press, 1998.

Hawking, Stephen W., *A Brief History of Time, From the Big Bang to Black Holes*, Bantam, 1998.

Hitchcock, John L., *The Web of the Universe: Jung, the "New Physics," and Human Spirituality, 1991.*

Irion, Robert, "Black Holes," *Smithsonian*, April 2008.

Koonz, Mark, "The Generosity of Thomas Forsyth Torrance: a memoir with letters," *The Princeton Theological Review*, Fall 2008.

Krauss, Lawrence M. and Glenn D. Starkman, "The Fate of Life in the Universe," *Scientific American*, November 1999.

Magee, Patrick, "The New Physics, Cosmology and Religion," Zephyr Point Presbyterian Conference Center, Lake Tahoe, California.

Masterpasqua, Frank, "Toward a Dynamical Developmental Understanding of Disorder," *The Psychological Meaning of Chaos: Translating Theory Into Practice*, American Psychological Association, 1997.

McGrath, Alister E., *Science and Religion: An Introduction*, Blackwell, 1999.

McTaggart, Lynne, *The Field*, Harper Perennial, 2002.

Peebles, P. James E., David N. Schramm, Edwin L. Turner and Richard G. Kron, "The Evolution of the Universe," *Scientific American Online*, July, 1998.

Primack, Joel R. and Nancy Ellen Abrams, *The View from the Center of the Universe: Discovering Our Extraordinary Place in the Cosmos*, Riverhead Books, 2006.

Purser, Ronald E., "Global Cyber-Tech and Integral Consciousness," XXV Annual Gebser Conference, October 1999.

Russell, Robert John, "Bridging Science and Religion: Why It Must Be Done," The Center for Theology and the Natural Sciences, Berkeley, California.

Schilling, Harold K., *The New Consciousness in Science and Religion*, United Church Press, 1973.

Serrone, Sue, "Starburst" (interview with Brian Swimme), *Festivals*, Vol. 6, No. 2.

Spong, John Shelby, *A New Christianity For a New World,* HarperSanFrancisco, 2001.

Spong, John Shelby, *Why Christianity Must Change or Die*, HarperSan Francisco, 1998.

Swimme, Brian and Thomas Berry, *The Universe Story: From the Primordial Flaring Forth to the Ecozoic Era*, HarperCollins, 1994.

Tolle, Eckhart, *A New Earth: Awakening to Your Life's Purpose*, Plume, 2006.

Weinberg, Steven, *The First Three Minutes, A Modern View of the Origin of the Universe*, Bantam, 1977.

Wells, Spencer, *The Journey of Man*, Random House, 2003.

Whitney, Donald S., "A Review of Eckhart Tolle's *A New Earth*," website of The Center for Biblical Spirituality, 2008.

Wilkens, Robert Louis, *The Myth of Christian Beginnings*, Wipf & Stock Publishers, 2009.

NOTES

[i] Jacques Monod.

[ii] James Gleick, "Have Meme, Will Travel," *Smithsonian,* May 2011.

[iii] These experiments were performed by Roger Nelson and referred to by Lynne McTaggart in *The Field.*

[iv] Wolfgang Giegerich, *The Soul's Logical Life: Towards a Rigorous Notion of Psychology,* New York, Peter Lang, 2001, p. 262.

[v] Peter Russell, in William Arntz, Betsy Chasse, and Mark Vicente, *What the Bleep Do We Know!?*: *Discovering the Endless Possibilities for Altering Your Everyday Reality,* Deerfield Beach, FL, Health Communications, 2007, p. 95.

[vi] Maharishi Mahesh, *What the Bleep Do We Know!?* p. 115.

[vii] William Tiller, *What the Bleep Do We Know!?* p. 242.

[viii] Arntz, Chasse, and Vicente, *What the Bleep Do We Know!?* p. 120.

[ix] Micael Ledwith in *What the Bleep Do We Know!?* pp. 247–248.

[x] Stuart Hameroff, *What the Bleep Do We Know!?* p. 161.

[xi] Lawrence M. Krauss and Glenn D. Starkman, "The Fate of Life in the Universe," *Scientific American,* November 1999.

[xii] P. James E. Peebles, David N. Schramm, Edwin L. Turner, and Richard G. Kron, "The Evolution of the Universe," in David Levy, Ed., *The Scientific American Book of the Cosmos,* p. 41.

[xiii] *What the Bleep Do We Know?* p. 239.

[xiv] William Saletan, "We've Made Our Match," *The Washington Post,* May 13, 2007.

[xv] Ray Kurzweil, author of *The Singularity Is Near.*

[xvi] Microprocessor chips are sometimes smaller than a micron. To put it in perspective, a human hair is 100 microns thick.

[xvii] Transistors are the tiny switches that manage the flow of electronic data.

[xviii] The process of "building active circuitry on the smallest scale that life itself uses."

[xix] Dharmendra Modha.

[xx] Brandon Bailey, "Team's Brainchild: PCs Like Us," *San Jose Mercury News*, November 18, 2009.

[xxi] Steve Johnson, "Intel Joins Search for Thought-Controlled Tech," *San Jose Mercury News*, January 17, 2010.

[xxii] Ibid.

[xxiii] Anita Silvers, chair of the philosophy department at San Francisco State University, quoted in "Intel Joins Search for Thought-Controlled Tech."

[xxiv] Ibid.

[xxv] The Davos Question, http://www.youtube.com/watch?v=BDqs-OZWw9o

[xxvi] Bruce Mehlman and Larry Irving, "Bring on the Exaflood, *The Washington Post,* May 24, 2007.

xxvii David Bank, quoted in "Losing Popularity Contest, MySpace Tries a Makeover," *The New York Times,* May 3, 2009.

xxviii Mark Zuckerberg, quoted in "Company on the Verge of a Social Breakthrough," *The New York Times,* June 7, 2010.

xxix Martha Anderson, quoted in "Twitter Archive at Library of Congress Could Help Redefine History's Scope," *The Washington Post,* May 6, 2010.

xxx David Sarno, "With Jobangels and Jobshouts, Twitter Helps Jobless Find Work," *Los Angeles Times,* February 10, 2009.

xxxi Elizabeth Drescher, quoted in "Social Media and the Seminary," *Currents Newsletter,* Spring 2010.

xxxii Darleen Pryds, associate professor at the Franciscan School of Theology, quoted in "Social Media and the Seminary."

xxxiii "Massively Collaborative Math," August 9, 2010, retrieved from htttp://www.drdobbs.com/tools/massively-collaborative-math/226600273

xxxiv Mary Cheney, daughter of Dick Cheney.

xxxv Marcus Barnes, "DVDs Key to Show's Sex-cess," *The Sun,* October 4, 2007.

xxxvi Roya Nikkhah, "NHS Tells School Children of Their 'Right' to 'an Orgasm a Day,'" *The Telegraph,* July 12, 2009.

xxxvii Isabel V. Sawhill, quoted in Blaine Harden, "Numbers Drop for the Married with Children," *The Washington Post,* March 4, 2007.

xxxviii Joe Rodriguez, "Firefighters Rescue Dog as Fire Destroys San Jose Home," *San Jose Mercury News*, August 30, 2009.

xxxix http://wikileaks.org/About.html

xl Jim Wunderman, president of the Bay Area Council of CEOs.

xli James MacPherson, quoted in "Reporting on Pasadena, from Mumbai Bureau," *The Denver Post*, May 11, 2007.

xlii Subhash Dhar, quoted in John Boudreau, *San Jose Mercury News*, December 5, 2006.

xliii Thomas L. Friedman, op-ed columnist, "The Inflection Is Near?" *The New York Times*, March 7, 2009.

xliv Amyris.

xlv Carla Shatz, head of Harvard's neurobiology department, quoted in "Hennessy Appoints Harvard Scientist to Lead Bio-X Program," *Stanford University News*, March 20, 2007.

xlvi "US: Stanford Prepares For Bookless Libraries," *University World News*, May 23, 2010.

xlvii "Now Playing: A Game That Wants You," redOrbit, February 21, 2007.

xlviii Lev Grossman, "You–Yes, You–Are Time's Person of the Year," *Time*, December 25, 2006.

xlix Julie Barko-Germany, Institute for Politics, Democracy and the Internet, George Washington University, in Elise Ackerman, "Sen. Clinton adds new twist to Web campaigns," *San Jose Mercury News*, January 25, 2007.

l Neal Gabler, *Los Angeles Times,* April 19, 2006.

138

li Joseph Buckley, quoted in Rachel Beck, "All Business: Investors Getting Heard," *The Washington Post*, February 16, 2007.

lii Fred Hyatt, "Are We Missing a Mideast Moment?" *The Washington Post,* May 8, 2011.

liii Christopher Drew and John Markoff, "Contractors Vie for Plum Work, Hacking for U.S.," *The New York Times,* May 30, 2009.

liv David Ignatius, quoted by Jason Horowitz, "We've Got a Visual," *The Washington Post,* May 5, 2011.

lv Mike McConnell, quoted by David Sanger, "US Sets the Pace in Race for Cyber Weapons," *The Age,* April 29, 2009.

lvi Max Boot, senior fellow for National Security Studies, Council on Foreign Relations, "The Changing Face of Warfare," a program hosted by World Affairs Council, November 6, 2006.

lvii Robin Wright, "Since 2001, a Dramatic Increase in Suicide Bombings," *The Washington Post*, April 18, 2008.

lviii Political theorist Yaron Ezrahi, quoted in Thomas L. Friedman, "Behind the Masks," *The New York Times*, June 20, 2007.

lix Dr. Daniel Perez, venture partner with a San Francisco investment firm, quoted in Steve Johnson, "'Brain Drain' Threatening Biotech Firms, Report Warns," *San Jose Mercury News*, December 6, 2006.

lx Seshan Rammohan, executive director of TiE Silicon Valley, quote in CarForums.com, retrieved from http://www.car-forums.com/talk/showthread.php?t=29766

[lxi] Frank Davies, "Survey: U.S. Losing its Edge in Innovation," *San Jose Mercury News*, June 16, 2009.

[lxii] Friedman, "Who's Sleeping Now?" *The New York Times,* January 9, 2010.

[lxiii] The Pew Research Center, *The 2008 Pew Global Attitudes Survey in China*, July 22, 2008.

[lxiv] The Washington Consensus refers to the free-market, pro-trade, and globalization policies promoted by the United States.

[lxv] Patrick J. Buchanan, "Auto Graveyard," February 16, 2007, retrieved from http://www.freerepublic.com

[lxvi] Steven Chu, U.S. energy secretary and Nobel Prize-winning physicist, quoted in Frank Davies, "Chu on Climate Threat: Earth Is Like the Titanic," *San Jose Mercury News*, April 8, 2009.

[lxvii] Friedman, "And the Color of the Year Is..." *The New York Times,* December 22, 2006.

[lxviii] The coalition includes Yahoo, Wal-Mart, Environmental Defense, U.S. Environmental Protection Agency, U.S. Energy Department, U.S. mayors, retailers, religious organizations, and conservation groups.

[lxix] "Energy-Efficient Lighting," *San Jose Mercury News*, February 22, 2007.

[lxx] Fred Krupp, quoted in Thomas L. Friedman, "Marching with a Mouse," *The New York Times*, March 16, 2007.

[lxxi] Ibid.

[lxxii] Friedman, "And the Color of the Year is . . ."

[lxxiii] Steven Chu.

[lxxiv] Arnold Schwarzenegger.

[lxxv] Tony Blair.

[lxxvi] Grasses or shrubs that grow on marginal land.

[lxxvii] Mike Leary, director of the National BioEnergy Center, part of the National Renewable Energy laboratory in Golden, Colorado, quoted in Suzanne Bohan, "Driving into the Future with Biofuels," *San Jose Mercury News*, May 2, 2009.

[lxxviii] Marla Dickerson, "Big Solar Projects Light Up Critics," *Los Angeles Times*, December 7, 2008.

[lxxix] One megawatt of electricity is usually enough to power 750 to 1,000 homes.

[lxxx] Brigitte Egger, in the newsletter of The Jung Society of Washington, September 5, 2008. Egger is a Jungian training analyst and ecologist in Zurich. She concentrates on the psychic and symbolic dimensions of collective issues, building up the field of psychecology.

[lxxxi] Elizabeth Kolbert (quoting a researcher at the Centers for Disease Control), "Why are we so fat?" *The New Yorker*, July 20, 2009.

[lxxxii] David A. Kessler, *The End of Overeating: Taking Control of the Insatiable American Appetite,* New York, Rodale, p. 145.

[lxxxiii] Francis Delpeuch, Bernard Maire, Emmanuel Monnier, and Michelle Holdsworth, *Globesity: A Planet Out of Control?* New York, Routledge, 2009, p. 33.

[lxxxiv] Paul Ehrlich, quoted in Sarah Jane Keller, "Q&A: Stanford's Paul Ehrlich Fears the Worst for a Planet with 7 Billion Residents," *Stanford University News*, October 26, 2011.

141

[lxxxv] "Strange Dark Energy Acts as Galactic Diet Enforcer," December 17, 2008, retrieved from http://www.usatoday.com/tech/science/space/2008-12-16-dark-energy_N.htm

[lxxxvi] Editorial, "the revenge of e.e. cummings," *Boston Globe*, April 29, 2008, retrieved from http://www.boston.com/bostonglobe/editorial_opinion/edit orials/articles/2008/04/29/the_revenge_of_ee_cummings/

[lxxxvii] Americans Elect intended to have its candidate on the ballot in all 50 states for the 2012 presidential election, but they were unable to find an agreed-upon candidate for that election.

[lxxxviii] Gary Small from UCLA, quoted in Melissa Healy, "Internet Use May Help You Search and Find...a Healthier Mind," *Los Angeles Times*, October 19, 2009.